Yolande's Atlanta

From the historical to the hysterical

Yolande Gwin

PEACHTREE PUBLISHERS, LTD.

Published by
PEACHTREE PUBLISHERS, LTD.
494 Armour Circle, N. E., Atlanta, Georgia 30324

Manufactured in the United States of America

Library of Congress Catalog Number: 83-61918

ISBN: 0-931948-43-6

Dedicated in loving memory
of my parents,
James and Marypearl Copley Gwin

Contents

Acknowledgements

SPECIAL THANKS are due to Patsy A. Wiggins and Jannelle Jones McRee, who sorted through boxes of collected material to compile the contents of this book; to Lillian Salter, who then typed it; to the *Atlanta Journal and Constitution* reference department, which researched dates and provided many photos; to Mrs. Dick Adair and Mrs. Charles Hurt, who encouraged me to go through with this project; and to John McKenzie, who designed the book jacket.

Y.G.

Foreword

A LL OF US who have worked on the newspapers in
Atlanta over the past forty years or so have looked upon
Yolande Gwin with affection and respect and more than a
trace of awe. She is today, as described by Sarah Dunbar in
Buckhead Atlanta, "the Grande Dame of Journalism." But
the "Grande Damerie" is based on the fact that she was and is,
and has been from the beginning, a hard-charging reporter,
with a concededly tough, inquiring mind behind an aura of
amiability. With a plenitude of human understanding, she
could cover any type of news story to which she was assigned,
and when assignments were slow in coming, she made her
own.

Being a maiden lady, she did not fall into the pattern of
many parental types, both male and female, who made a
journalistic living by writing about the joys and tribulations
of childbearing and childraising. She chose instead to view
the family as a social unit, and to describe Atlanta and its
people in their relations to each other on the social level,
joined or separated on the bases of family background,
income, education, church and club memberships, and social
interests.

Thus she became identified to many as purely a "society reporter," describing debut parties at the Piedmont Driving Club or the Phoenix Society, and publishing the good works done in the public interest by ladies and gentlemen well known to all.

There was, for example, a saying around the office, "If Yoley didn't cover it, it didn't happen." This, of course, was not an exaggeration, as this book will amply demonstrate.

However, she has not been, and is not now, merely a writer of social chatter. She is a historian, telling the story of Atlanta social development, not in the dust-dry prose of the historian, but with the lively wit and humor of a newspaper columnist.

Yolande's Atlanta opens with an essay on Atlanta in the thirties, which she calls the brightest social decade in the city's history. She brings us an affectionate picture of her city as the homeplace of *Gone With the Wind*, with glimpses of the world of Peggy Mitchell and Tara. There are personal touches, about people, places and things Yolande has known and loved. And there are revealing stories of Yolande herself, of the Grande Dame who moves into her golden years still merry and bright and brave. And in doing so, making all of us who read her book feel brighter and more cheerful.

Robyn Peeples Walsh, one of Yolande's contemporaries in the early days of the *Atlanta Constitution*, remembers her as a "darling person, a natural, sweet, dear person, a very special, unique person." And all of these qualities shine through in the pages of this book.

Harold Martin
Atlanta, Georgia
September, 1983

Introduction

IT WAS A spring day shortly after my graduation from Washington Seminary. Several friends and I were playing bridge and munching fudge at an afternoon tea, when one of them (Runa Erwin, now Mrs. Fred Ware of Augusta) said that she had decided not to accept a summer job in the society department of the *Atlanta Georgian* newspaper. My eyes grew wide, and I made her repeat it; I couldn't believe my ears. I think I was born with ink in my blood, and the thought of actually working at a newspaper thrilled me.

The next day I went to see Mrs. W. C. Jarnigan, who was society editor of the paper and wrote a popular column called "Polly Peachtree." As soon as she received me, she told me to get on the phone and call around town for some news. I called everyone I knew and many people I didn't know but had read their names in the newspaper. Well, I must have done all right, because I got the job!

At the end of the summer, I was offered a permanent position. I was so excited that I walked around the corner to Rich's and bought myself an ice cream soda to celebrate. Even though I had signed up to attend Sweet Briar, I loved working at the newspaper and wanted to continue doing so. I hurried home to tell my parents the good news. My mother was instantly delighted and proud of me, but my father was less than enthusiastic. "You cannot accept the job," he said. "No Gwin daughter was ever allowed to work. They stayed home or went to college. My answer is no." I begged again and again before bedtime, but made little progress. Finally my mother came to my rescue. She told my father that I would be working with some nice ladies (both of them knew Mrs. Jarnigan) and that I would be living at home with them. The thought of my living at home made him happy, so he finally relented and said, "Well, just for one year you can work."

More than fifty years later, my newspaper career is still going strong. And my father, like my mother, came to be very proud of me.

During those fifty-plus years, I have seen Atlanta society from the inside. I have debuted as a member of the Atlanta Debutante Club, interviewed celebrities ranging from Clark Gable and Vivien Leigh to J. Edgar Hoover, and talked my way past more than one policeman to get a story. In the pages which follow, you will read many of the stories behind those stories which appeared in the *Atlanta Journal and Constitution*. You'll remember things you thought were forgotten. You'll learn a little history about Atlanta—my city. And I hope we'll even share a laugh or two. From the historical to the hysterical, here is *Yolande's Atlanta*.

Yolande's Atlanta

The Thrilling Thirties

A Time of Hats and White Gloves

ATLANTA HAD HER roaring twenties and her fabulous forties and fifties, but the thrilling thirties was an era packed with excitement and social happenings. I believe it was the grandest decade in Atlanta's social history.

Often called the years of hats and white gloves, the thirties brought life back to the victims of the market crash of '29. Mr. and Mrs. Edward Inman had just moved into their elegant residence on Andrews Drive which they had named Swan House. Throughout Atlanta, other handsome homes were built. These soon, like the more established homes, became the places for social gatherings. There was a great deal of home entertaining in those days—afternoon bridge parties, teas, and seated dinners. Fancy paper lanterns or candles lighted open porches for formal and informal parties during the spring and summer months.

Despite the big city dreams of local leaders and officials, Atlanta was still neighborly. Everybody went "downtown," and Nunnally's popular ice cream parlor and candy store on Peachtree Street, facing Luckie Street, was where Atlantans met their dates and gathered after the movies. The Metropolitan Theater was across the street, and anyone who

Margaret Palmer in Scarlett's dress, escorted by Harry Sommers

was anybody had to be seen downtown at midday, in the afternoons, or at night. In the evening, Peachtree became Atlanta's own Great White Way of movie houses—the Metropolitan, the Paramount, the Georgia, the Capitol, the Grand, the Howard—whose marquee lights twinkled like so many stars.

The really big excitement in showplaces had come just prior to the thrilling thirties, when "The Fabulous Fox" opened on Christmas day of 1929. Aside from its entertainment greatness and its contribution to the lifestyle of the city, the Fox had another distinction. It was where dating couples went to watch a movie amid a romantic setting, and to hold hands as stars glittered among clouds rolling overhead in the fantastic interior of the Fox. Hundreds of Atlanta men popped *the* question in this theater. Many young girls were taken to the Fox on their first dates. It is as much a part of Atlanta as City Hall. For years the week-long visit by the Metropolitan Opera brought glamour to the Fox. As many as could obtain tickets were there in evening clothes, with white tie and tails. Going to the Fox was the thing to do.

But the thrilling thirties were not all play and fun. There was achievement, too. Atlanta's Bobby Jones was golfdom's greatest that year. He won the fabled "Grand Slam" by finishing first in the British Open and Amateur, and the U.S. Open and Amateur tournaments. He returned to a hero's welcome in Atlanta and brought worldwide fame to his club, the East Lake Country Club.

The thrilling thirties were dancing years, too. The regular Saturday night dances at the Piedmont Driving Club took place on the terrace during the summer and inside, naturally, during the winter. Late summer afternoons and early evenings, everyone vied for a table under "the big tree"—the big oak at the southwest side of the terrace whose heavy limbs were like caressing arms around the area. Since the Driving Club is located on the site of the farm of the late B. F. Walker, the big tree began its life with hens roosting in it. When the old tree had to be cut down some years ago, sentimental club members rushed to get souvenirs of bark and wood. Footstools, tables, etc., have been made from the "remains."

During the thirties, the back porch at the club, overlooking Piedmont Park, was a favorite place for parties. In those years, the "bride's table" was the important part of the wedding reception. The newlyweds and their wedding attendants dined at an elaborate table and enjoyed a delicious dinner with frequent champagne toasts. Reception guests, hosts, and families mingled in the ballroom. The club's side porch overlooking the swimming pool was also a popular setting for parties. Women wore large, floppy hats. All of this was, of course, before air conditioning.

The city's oldest Jewish social club, the Standard Club, moved in 1929 to its "new home" on Ponce de Leon Avenue and continued its round of social events. Thomas B. Paine, the city's courtly gentleman who led the debutante cotillions at the Driving Club, continued to be popular at all leading social affairs.

Members of the Capital City Club and their guests dined and danced in the moonlight on the roof garden of the downtown club, as well as on the terrace at the country club. The al fresco affairs soon disappeared, the victims of air conditioning. The club's famous and popular Mirador Room, encircled with mirrors featuring bird paintings by the noted artist Athos Menaboni, was the site of many gala parties.

Roof-garden dancing was also featured atop the downtown Atlanta Athletic Club, a city landmark for years; the country club at East Lake had a large terrace overlooking the lake where boating as well as swimming was enjoyed. Air

[6]

conditioning brought an end to these fun days and nights.

The Druid Hills Golf Club was, and still is, a great place for society to dine and dance. It, too, had a wide terrace. When the Met came here, the barbecues at the club were highlights for the opera stars. Druid Hills also was one of the most popular places for college fraternity dances, as was the Capital City Country Club.

Fraternity houses at Tech had their tea dances after the football games. Fraternities and sororities at Tech and Boys' High School and at Washington Seminary had dances at the Shrine Mosque at the Fox, as well as at many clubs. Atlantans were also getting a taste of afternoon tea dances at the newly opened Biltmore Hotel.

People were humming and singing popular Cole Porter songs such as "Night and Day," "I Get a Kick Out of You," "Begin the Beguine," and "Just One of Those Things." And everybody learned to dance from Margaret Bryan.

During all these years, the handsome Swan House, the home of Mr. and Mrs. Edward Inman on Andrews Drive, stood in dignified beauty. Mr. Inman died a few years after moving in from their former home on Fifteenth Street in Ansley Park, now the site of handsome townhouses.

The stately Mrs. Inman gave beautiful parties at her home, one of the most elegant and handsome homes in the city. One time a luncheon was planned for sixty guests. The evening before, Mrs. Inman was upstairs and heard a tremendous and loud crash. Then there was silence. An awful car accident somewhere, she thought. The next morning, the servants gave her the real story; the entire ceiling of the library had fallen to the floor. Being the perfect hostess, with plenty of savoir-faire, she just closed off the library and the guests were none the wiser.

But these aspects of Atlanta society were merely the backdrop of the grandest decade in our social history. Center stage was held unquestionably by the world premiere of the movie verson of Margaret Mitchell's *Gone With the Wind*. Her book had been published three years earlier (1936) and within weeks had become the nation's best seller. Then in mid-December of 1939, the movie premiered at the Loew's Grand. That week, I would have to say, was the pinnacle of Atlanta's social life. Clark Gable, Vivien Leigh, Olivia de Havilland, Butterfly McQueen, and many other stars of the movie attended parties around town. The grand parade along Peachtree Street was seen by more people than were in the combined armies of Generals Hood, Johnston, and Sherman during the Battle of Atlanta. A top social event during the festivities was the *Gone With the Wind* costume ball at the city auditorium, sponsored by the Atlanta Junior League, which was headed that year by Mrs. W. Colquitt Carter. Official hosts of the ball were Gov. E. D. Rivers; *Atlanta Constitution* editor Clark Howell, Jr., who was master of cereronies; and Atlanta mayor William B. Hartsfield, who was chairman. Preliminary music was provided by Enrico Liede, while Kay Kyser and his orchestra provided dance music.

A contest of sorts had been held among Atlanta debutantes prior to the ball to decide who would wear one of Scarlett O'Hara's gowns to the ball. Margaret Palmer (now Mrs. Earl Cecil Moses of Greatbend, Kansas) was the lucky winner, and on the night of the ball she led the Grand March with Rhett Butler (Clark Gable). She wore the green-sprigged mousseline gown worn by Scarlett (Vivien Leigh) in the movie.

The ball was a never-to-be-forgotten event, especially for Mildred Hartsfield, the mayor's daughter. She had been selected to sit in a box seat between Gable and his wife, Carole Lombard. During the evening, Miss Hartsfield discovered she had lost one of her earrings. The three searched the floor of the box but could not find the earring. Early the next day, a messenger knocked at Miss Hartsfield's door and handed her a small box. Inside was a pair of earrings with a note that said, "My dear Mildred, We hope you like these and that they will take the place of the one you lost." It was signed, "Carole and Clark Gable."

It was natural that *Gone With the Wind*, both the book and the movie, would inspire parties. The first for an Atlanta debutante was the weekend house party given by Mrs. Peter Walton Godfrey at her antebellum home in nearby Madison for Robyn Peeples, daughter of the late Mr. and Mrs. Edwin Peeples. (She is now Mrs. Frank Walsh.) She made her bow in the 1937-1938 season, and this party was given in the fall of 1937. It was a costume affair, with all the guests being given attire as worn by guests at the barbecue at Twelve Oaks. Mrs. Godfrey's house guests rode horseback, went buggy riding, and attended square dances, tea parties, and a corn-husking party. It was one of the hits of that debutante season.

Gone With the Wind, of course, was a hit for all seasons.

Yolande's Atlanta

Gone With the Wind
Madness

Constitution *Printed First News of Peggy's Book, February 9, 1936*

HARD-PRESSED for a story one day, I called Peggy Mitchell and, just for the spirit of the thing, asked if the "Great American Novel" she had been rumored as writing for years had ever been completed.

Her answer was the first story ever written on *Gone With the Wind*. It appeared in the *Constitution* on February 9, 1936, five months prior to publication of the book.

All newspapermen and women dream of someday writing the Great American Novel, and Peggy Mitchell was no exception. She had used "my book" as an excuse (everyone thought) for leaving parties early, for declining invitations, and for any other apology of the moment.

As casual as the breeze, Peggy discussed the book and its forthcoming publication in June of that year. My story is reprinted here:

"To an already distinguished list of Atlanta authors, we take exceptional pride today in adding the name of Margaret Mitchell, whose book, *Gone With the Wind*, is scheduled for spring publication. The author, better known as Peggy, is a journalist of unusual talent and note, and her forthcoming book will present an interesting and charmingly prepared piece of work which will have wide appeal, especially in the South.

"In naming her book *Gone With the Wind*, Peggy caught and presented to the public a concise portrayal of facts and events which, in a true sense of the word, are *gone with the wind,* never to come again in the same tempo. But they are forever recalled along with the pathos of that never-to-be-forgotten decade, the stirring days of the sixties.

"Enshrined with hallowed memories of a lost cause, records already mellowed with age depict the war-torn days of the Civil War. The scenes were laid in the vicinity of Atlanta between 1860 and 1873 and represent three major periods of that era—pre-war days, the years of the war, and Reconstruction days—which are tempered with historical facts and characters.

"Miss Mitchell has written not a war book but a novel, presenting a cross-section of life of the times and giving a realistic picture of how people in all walks of life, even including Yankee carpetbaggers, reacted to the catastrophe that befell them. The author verified her facts through extensive research and study. As aforementioned, her book is not a war story, from the standpoint of reference, but is a historical novel which will occupy a prominent place in leading public and private libraries.

"In private life, Peggy is Mrs. John Marsh and is the daughter of Eugene Mitchell (who has since died) and the late Mrs. Mitchell, prominent pioneer Atlantans. Her clever pen is fortified with an extensive knowledge of literature and a wide vocabulary which equip her for the art of writing on any subject. In years past, her humorous viewpoint gave her newspaper feature articles wide interest. This column takes this opportunity to congratulate the clever young writer on her literary effort, and joins with countless other friends in anticipation of the release date."

Several months later as the publication date neared, Davison's department store and Mrs. Luise Sims, head of the book department, were offered the pre-publication party by the MacMillan Publishing Company. Mr. Raymond Kline, then president of Davison's, called in Mrs. John Knox (now Mrs. Leonard P. Eager of Evansville, Wisconsin), who was doing public relations work, to discuss the party. Mr. Kline asked Mrs. Knox if the store should have a small party or go all out. Mrs. Knox recalls that she answered, "I have known Peggy Mitchell always, and I don't believe she could write anything earth-shattering. I think we should have a small party in the book department, run a small ad in the newspaper, and let her autograph her book if anyone comes." Mrs. Knox also suggested that the store should discount the price of the book, which was $3.00, to $2.75 for the day of the party. I attended that first party along with my parents. It was a small gathering, but it was certainly a historic event.

The Georgia of
Gone With the Wind

June, 1937

A YOUNG WOMAN who made literary history has inadvertently brought thousands of visitors to Georgia.

She is Margaret Mitchell, author of the world-famous and now Pulitzer Prize-winning novel, *Gone With the Wind*.

They come from north, east, south, and west. They come by plane and by train, but more often by motor, in an effort to fully cover the historic spots which have made the nation Georgia-conscious since Miss Mitchell's book was published.

Their questions and their requests are always the same. They want to go to Jonesboro. They want to see Tara and Twelve Oaks, and they want to gaze upon the paths and byways where Scarlett and the Tarleton twins rode horseback in the lazy summer afternoons before the war clouds appeared above the peaceful tranquility of the Old South.

In Atlanta it is the same. At the offices of The Atlanta Historical Society, where Miss Ruth Blair[1] is executive director, there are as many as one hundred requests a day from

---

[1] Executive Director, 1937-1956.

visitors for sightseeing trips throughout the city to spots made famous by Miss Mitchell's book.

They want to see Miss Pittypat's house. They want to see the Union Station where the wounded soldiers lay dying for want of medical attention. They want to see the exact site of the Battle of Atlanta, and to know if there are any breastworks left. Where was Scarlett's lumber mill? Where was the home of Scarlett and Rhett Butler? That of Ashley and Melanie? Belle Watling's on Decatur Street? Peachtree and Marietta streets? Five Points?

Atlanta, Jonesboro, and Five Points; Peachtree, Decatur, and Marietta Streets; the Union Station, and the actions and events are history. Tara, Twelve Oaks, and the other houses, and all the characters, however, are fictional. The people and the houses are typical of people and houses of the period and the locality, but none of them is modeled after actual people or houses.

Georgia is blessed in that there still remain many homes which are far-famed as the few remaining shrines of that gracious charm which history associates with the Old South. In them that grand old tradition is still carried on. In them the present-day *Gone With the Wind* visitor sees the Old South in its true manner and in the same way in which it was portrayed by Miss Mitchell in her book.

The Old South lives again within the walls of these old homes, and it is in them that visitors may envision the actions of the characters in *Gone With the Wind*. But the tour must be only a mythical one to Tara, to Twelve Oaks, to Miss Pittypat's, and to the other homes so often referred to in the book. In her extensive research after acceptance of her book, Miss Mitchell went to considerable trouble to locate Tara at a point in the country where there was no house, and to locate Aunt Pittypat's house on what was a vacant lot during that period in history.

As for the historic sites mentioned in the book, the movements of the armies, the actions of the Yankee soldiers, and the sufferings of the Confederate soldiers, there is no doubt of their veracity. Diaries, histories, and old newspapers support the latter as an everlasting contradiction to the flood of rumors which, unfortunately, have been rampant, to the effect that the author overdescribed the desperate and and devastating conditions which the South was forced to accept from the Northern armies.

That the various points mentioned in the book are historically accurate is evidenced by the fact that plans are now under way to place seventy to one hundred temporary wooden markers to commemorate the Battle of Atlanta. This project is a direct result of Miss Mitchell's book, and will eventually place one hundred seventy markers as it helps to develop a history-conscious citizenry.

Itineraries are planned for visitors whose interest in the city's historic sites has been aroused by the novel, and attractive folders briefly presenting the city's history will be prepared. Policemen, especially, will be educated to direct visitors to scenes of interest.

Since the book was published, Miss Mitchell has received thousands of letters and telephone calls from tourists who want to locate the battlefield of Peachtree Creek and other battles fought in and around Atlanta. Attendance has more than doubled at the Cyclorama, the painting showing the Battle of Atlanta on July 22, 1864. It is a work of historical, artistic, and mechanical importance, so critical to the book that even Atlantans are reviving their interest in it.

The Mitchell home at 1401 Peachtree is one of the first places a visitor wants to see. It is the home of Eugene and Stephens Mitchell,[2] father and brother of the author. The

---

[2] 1401 Peachtree Street is now the site of an office building. Eugene Mitchell died on June 16, 1944. Stephens Mitchell died on May 12, 1983.

latter and her husband, John R. Marsh,[3] public relations counsel of the Georgia Power Company, reside in an apartment a scant block away from the parental roof. Somehow the Mitchell home on Peachtree gives a breath of the Old South, that fleeting atmosphere which visitors come here to feel. Southern mansions in and near Atlanta, including the famous Mimosa Hall in Roswell, have been the mecca for tourists who desire to see a home with a real Southern appearance.

Georgians, of course, are familiar with the scenes in the book, but it has nevertheless inspired these same Georgians to dig down into their history books for more accurate information to pass along to the world when she comes rolling into the state behind her steering wheel.

Jonesboro, in Clayton County, is the scene of part of the book, so the town has attracted thousands of visitors looking for Tara and Twelve Oaks. They all believe the famous old landmark Tara still stands, so vividly has Miss Mitchell painted it.

The historic publicity which Atlanta and Georgia have received from *Gone With the Wind* is unparalleled in the annals of the state and has provided inspiration and information to millions. The book has received the congratulations of the Georgia Senate in a resolution unanimously adopted by the upper branch of the Assembly.

The resolution was signed by Senate President John Spivey and by Senators Atkinson of Savannah, Millican of Atlanta, McCutchen of Dalton, and Williams of Waycross. Senator Atkinson, before asking the passing of the resolution, pointed out that it is the only major book in recent years which truly depicts life of the Old South.

Miss Mitchell has done more than write a famous novel.

---

[3] John R. Marsh died in 1952.

[19]

The historical background she presents has brought to light many facts which rumor and legend have distorted and which haste and carelessness have changed into serious misstatements.

Visitors to Georgia, supplied with guidebooks and thirsty for background for the adventures of Scarlett and Rhett, Melanie and Ashley, and all the other characters, have only to get into their cars and begin to tour. In their imaginations, these tourists will see Georgia as the world of Scarlett O'Hara, who is paramount in the world of fictional heroines. They will ride up and down Peachtree and live again in the days when the handsome and dashing Captain Rhett Butler rode horseback with his little daughter, Bonnie.

That same Peachtree stands today as one of the thoroughfares of the world. That same Georgia remains, of which Miss Mitchell wrote.

Petite Atlantan Meets Film Stars for the First Time

December 16, 1939

THE MAN WHO put four million dollars into filming *Gone With the Wind* and the principal stars who put their hearts into it met the author of the book for the first time yesterday afternoon.

Petite Margaret Mitchell, quiet of voice and smiling somewhat reservedly save at rare moments, gave her hand to David O. Selznick, the producer; to Clark Gable, Vivien Leigh, Evelyn Keyes, Ann Rutherford, and Laura Hope Crews, of the cast; and to Carole Lombard, Gable's glamorous wife, at a cocktail party of the Atlanta Women's Press Club.

Said Mr. Gable, "Do you suppose I could have a few words with her? After all, there is a lot I want to tell her."

Said Margaret Mitchell, "Isn't he grand! Just what I expected."

Said Carole Lombard, "Clark has been dying to meet you, Miss Mitchell."

Said Miss Vivien Leigh, "I think she is perfectly marvelous."

It all took place in a room eighteen feet by eleven feet.

Yolande's stories captured the excitement of the world premiere

There was another room and the bar, into which guests overflowed.

Peggy Mitchell had the spotlight and stole the scene. The greatest names of Hollywood gave it to her willingly. Gable only wanted to talk to Peggy Mitchell, and Gable, as in all his movie roles, found a way to get his girl.

They disappeared into a private dining room of the club at 5:16 o'clock. The door was locked. There Gable and Miss Mitchell talked over many things. Both refused to repeat what was said. The world would like to know the things they talked about, but probably never will.

Minutes slipped by, but Peggy and "Rhett" were still in conference. The clock showed 5:25. Most of the club members were getting a little nervous. What were they saying? Was she telling him she had him in mind for her character when she wrote the book?

When they came out, Peggy joined Vivien Leigh and Laura Hope Crews (Aunt Pittypat) in the main room. She confided to them, "If I sit up too straight, think nothing of it. Somebody jerked a chair back too far today, and I sat down too hard on the floor. Now I'm wrapped in adhesive tape."

Carole Lombard slipped into a chair beside her.

Soon Miss Mitchell's husband, John Marsh, beckoned it was time to leave.

It was nearing six o'clock. Louis B. Mayer held her coat for her. Mrs. Mayer was there, and goodbyes were said. The guests were leaving. Miss Mitchell gave a farewell wave to Mr. and Mrs. Gable, who left by the side terrace entrance. Miss Mitchell left by the front door.

Claudette Colbert remained to entertain guests.

"I hate to leave all this. Did Miss Mitchell have to leave so soon? Does she come to all the press club parties? Is she always as friendly as she was tonight?" asked Miss Colbert.

The crowd drank the remaining mint juleps.

Among the guests were Mrs. Selznick; Jock Whitney; Laurence Olivier; Miss Ona Munson; Miss Alicia Rhett; Louis B. Mayer; Robert Samuels; Mrs. Sidney Howard; John F. Wharton; Mr. and Mrs. Daniel T. O'Shea; W. R. Ferguson; Mr. and Mrs. E. B. Coleman; Mr. and Mrs. Herbert Bayard Swope; Mr. and Mrs. Charles Payson; Mr. and Mrs. Robert Lehman; Mr. and Mrs. Barklie Henry; Mr. and Mrs. Howard Dietz; Howard Strickling; Major and Mrs. Lenox R. Lohr; W. F. Rodgers; T. J. Connors; Mr. and Mrs. James Barrett; Mr. and Mrs. George Brett, Jr.; Mr. and Mrs. R. M. Brett; H. S. Lathem; Mr. and Mrs. A. J. Blanton; Mr. and Mrs. Allan Taylor; Miss Susan Myrick; Mrs. Julia Peterkin; Miss Inez Robb; Miss Marjorie Kinnan Rawlings; former Governor and Mrs. James M. Cox; Mr. and Mrs. James M. Cox, Jr.; W. S. Kirkpatrick, Nate Noble, and John Paschal, godfathers of the club; Mrs. W. S. Kirkpatrick; Mrs. Nate Noble; Mr. and Mrs. Wilbur Kurtz, Sr.; Mr. and Mrs. Stephens Mitchell; Mr. and Mrs. Norman Berg; Mr. and Mrs. Lucien Harris, Jr.; Miss Margaret Baugh; John A. Brice; Major and Mrs. Clark Howell; Mr. and Mrs. Randolph A. Hearst; and Edwin Pentecost.

Gone With the Wind
Reminiscences

IN MARCH OF 1981 I joined Jack Spalding, former editor of the *Atlanta Journal* and one of my favorite people, on a program for the Atlanta Historical Society. We discussed many things about Atlanta that night, and as always *Gone With the Wind* was one of the main topics. Following is an excerpt from the dialogue that evening:

JACK: Yolande has covered every sort of story imaginable. . . .I think the one she enjoyed most, however, was the premiere of *Gone With the Wind*. She was there and I was there, along with a few other people. What do you remember most about that, besides Vivien Leigh's lipstick?

YOLANDE: Yes, you were there then. Jack was doing the main story, and I was doing what in the newspaper business we call a sidebar story, which is the feature story. So we got to the Georgian Terrace, where Mr. Selznick was having a party for the stars, and we got there ahead of time, and I thought we were at the wrong place. I said, "I don't see a bar; this can't be right." Jack said, "Oh, yes, it is." So we were just sitting there, and there were newspaper people from all over the United States here, because it was quite an event, as you

Laurence Olivier tells Yolande a lot more than he intended to

all know—the premiere of *Gone With the Wind*. And newspaper people were just spilling out everywhere. So Jack and I were in there. He was looking out the window at Peachtree and all the people, and I was just sitting there on the couch thinking about what I was going to write.

So this woman came bouncing in and sat down by me and said, "Hey," and I said, "Hey." I thought she was another reporter. And so we just sat there. Finally she turned to me and she said, "Can I borrow your lipstick?" And I said, "No!" I said, "That's just like my toothbrush; you can't have my lipstick." She said, "Well, mine's in my purse and I don't have it, and I look horrible." I said, "Well, here's a Kleenex. Use it and then wipe it off real good." So she used it, then wiped it off and put it back. She said, "Thanks." I said, "You're welcome." We sat there some more, and in a few minutes this man roared in—it was Selznick; I recognized him from his pictures. He said, "Vivien, where in the hell have you been!" And here I was sitting right next to Vivien Leigh and didn't know it, didn't recognize her. Well, she didn't look like she did as Scarlett—that's why I didn't. We weren't good friends, anyway, even though she used my lipstick.

Well, as the party continued, other people kept coming in, and, oh, the place was just like that! Then who should come in but Laurence Olivier, so I thought to myself, "Well, now I've got Scarlett and the lipstick in my mind." I never carry a pencil if I can help it, because if someone sees you sitting with a paper and pencil they are not going to open their mouth; so I wedged my way over, and I have a picture to prove it, talking to Laurence Olivier. And I said, "Well, I'm glad you came today." And he said, "Well, I'm glad you came, too. Where are you from?" I said, "Oh, out there somewhere." And I said, "I want to ask you a question. Are you going to marry Vivien Leigh?" He was traveling with her, you know—he wasn't in the movie. And he said, "As soon as I get a divorce from my wife." I said, "You naughty boy, you. Anyway, I've got to get back to the bar." I was holding an empty glass. I skipped the bar and went to the lobby and called the office. At that time I was on the *Constitution* and I had to make the next day's paper, so I called the city editor and told him that Laurence Olivier was going to marry Vivien Leigh when he got the divorce. And he said, "Well, that's just fine, but when are you going to get your story written?" That's Pop Hines. He's the newspaperman that always wore the eyeshade like they have in the movies. I said, "Well, I'll be there in a little while." Of course, I finally got down there and wrote the story, and on the front page the next morning there was a little piece, "Olivier admits he's going to marry Vivien Leigh."

That afternoon there was another party—the whole week was nothing but parties. This one was downstairs in the ballroom of the old Georgian Terrace. I went down the receiving line, and when I got to Olivier he said, "Oh, *you* are the one who put that in the paper about me. Ohhh, I'm going to kill you!" I said, "Well, honey, let's don't do it now and ruin the party; do you want me to correct it and deny it in tomorrow's paper? I'll be glad to do it if you are mad." He said, "No! Just keep quiet about it and get away!" That was all right with me.

The grand thing was, the Atlanta Women's Press Club, of which that year I was the chairman for the party, so of course I had to have the money; well, I mean I didn't have the money, but I had everybody else's money—we gave a party at the Driving Club for Peggy Mitchell because Peggy had been a member of the Women's Press Club. So I was going out to cover the story, the photographer and I, and I didn't wear my badge, because, as I said, with paper and a pencil and a badge, too, you're not going to get any news. So we got to the

Driving Club and there were cars all up and down and just mashes of people and policemen. We went tearing up the street through an entrance—it was different from what it is now; they've redecorated and remodeled the club—but, anyway, there was a policeman who said, "I'm sorry, but you all can't go in; this is a private party." And I said, "Well, officer,"—I think I called him a captain; that made him feel good for a *minute*—I said, "Well, captain, I'm a member of this group that is giving the party. I have the money here to pay for the party." And he said, "That's a likely story, lady, but you still can't go in." And I argued with him, and the photographer argued, and he said, "No, no, no," and he waved at some traffic, "Come on by," he said. "You all go on."

I happened to think, and I told the photographer, "Are you game to go in the ladies' room with me?" And he said, "Any time, baby," and so we walked up Piedmont Avenue—I happened to know where there was another entrance to the Driving Club which was the servants' entrance. So we walked on up Piedmont Road, northward, and came to this entrance. And I said, "We are going in here." He said, "But this is the kitchen." I said, "Well, that might be better—we can get something to eat. Come on."

It was a balmy day. We walked on down to the side of the club where the windows to the ladies' room were, and I said, "Now this is what we are going to do. You stand up on your camera and open the window, and then I'll stand on the camera and you can push me in, and then you come on in." He gave me the funniest look and said, "Well, if you think that's all right, it's all right with me." So he gave me a push on my behind and then he gave me a pat and said, "Are you in?" And I said, "I'm in," so he came in and we sailed into the ballroom for the party and he got this picture. It is the first meeting between Clark Gable, Vivien Leigh and Peggy

Mitchell. My story and his picture ran on the front page of the *Constitution* the morning after that party. . . .

JACK: That was the first premiere. Do you remember the first anniversary of the premiere? Vivien and Olivier came back, and the plane couldn't land. Charlie Golson was the pilot, and they circled over the Grand with searchlights playing, and the crowd was waiting, and they went round and round. We'd get these radio reports. Ernest Rogers and Deezie Scott were flying with them; they were the accompanying press. Finally they put down in Augusta. Were they married then?

YOLANDE: No, no, they hadn't married. Because he hadn't quite gotten rid of or killed off his other wife.

JACK: They certainly went steady for a while.

YOLANDE: At the party that Mr. and Mrs. Alfred Kennedy gave—this is when they lived on Habersham Way—Vivien Leigh was holding court in the back room, the only woman in the back room, surrounded by men, and she was telling the worst jokes you ever heard. Somebody came out and told me about it, and said, "Don't go in there. She's telling dirty jokes. Stay out here with Olivia de Havilland, who is a lady." She was in another room holding court. But I remember all that, yes.

And then when the movie came out, it just went wild all over the country, you know. And some bus line in Atlanta decided they would take tours to Tara. So Peggy Mitchell, being such a mischievous little darling anyway, decided she'd ride down with them one day. So this busload of people, with Peggy right there, started down to Jonesboro, and the driver was just going along. He said, "We're nearly there; we're nearly there!" And we got into Jonesboro and he said, "Now, right down here on the right, in just a little while now, we'll get there." And somebody said, "What's on the right?" And he said, "We're not there yet, but right ahead of us is that little bridge," and some woman on the bus said, "What little bridge?" And he said, "You know, the little bridge where Scarlett and Melanie and the baby hid when they were going back to Tara. We'll be going over it in just a minute." Everyone was hanging outside of the bus and somebody said, "Well, I don't see it," and he said, "Well, you know, they must have redone this street, because that is where that bridge was." So they went on a little bit farther and he said, "Now we are coming up to Tara, it's right up there on the hill. You all look up there, Tara's right up there." And everybody hung out the bus window, you know, and this same woman said, "I don't see it," and he said, "Well, it's all those trees up there; it's summertime and all the trees are in bloom, that's why you can't see it. That's all right, you'll see Twelve Oaks next," and he went on down the road. "Now right over here on the left as we make this turn is Twelve Oaks. It's a beautiful place." And as he went on talking about Twelve Oaks, everybody hung out the window. He said, "Well, I declare, you know they've built a lot of things down here and I think they've built something right in front of Twelve Oaks."

So they finally got back to Atlanta and Peggy let everybody get off the bus and she walked up to the driver and said, "I certainly did enjoy this trip." He said, "Well, thank you so much, lady." She said, "I'm Margaret Mitchell." He said, "I'm so glad to know you. I'm Rhett Butler. . . ."

JACK: My great memory of *Gone With the Wind* was, I was making fifteen dollars a week on the *Constitution*, or maybe the federal minimum wage law did pass by then, and I got an automatic raise up to seventeen-fifty. It was one of those . . . What was Selznick's PR man's name? Birdsong, Birdworld?

[31]

He offered me a job at one hundred dollars a week, but it was just temporary—that was my great memory of that time, that and Olivia de Havilland arriving at the ball. Remember?

YOLANDE: Oh, she was such a grand lady.

JACK: Well, they had left her behind at the hotel, and everybody was seated and the thing was going on, and Major Howell was master of ceremonies. He was up on the stage having a fine time, and in came the assistant manager of the Georgian Terrace with Olivia de Havilland on his arm. They came sweeping down the aisle to the right, you remember how the old auditorium was, the old horseshoe boxes, big show. I met her later in Hollywood as part of my World War II experiences, and I asked about that. I said, "Was that staged or was that natural?" She said it really happened. I had always thought that it had been staged.

YOLANDE: It could have been; they'll do anything for publicity.

Gone With the Wind
Reunion Party

August 26, 1974

REMEMBER IN THE book and in the movie of *Gone With the Wind*, Scarlett took down the green velvet draperies in the parlor at Tara to make a dress to wear to Atlanta to see Rhett Butler?

And Rhett had been jailed by the Yankees. Remember?

Well, keep on remembering, but keep this in the back of your head. In the MGM movie version of this great book by Atlanta's Margaret Mitchell, the dress was made before the draperies, even to the tassel tiebacks.

Walter Plunkett, one of Hollywood's foremost designers, flew here recently to attend a reunion luncheon given by MGM at the Diplomat. He designed every costume Scarlett wore in the movie. The luncheon was a forerunner of the current showing of the Oscar-winning movie.

"The major point in the drapery dress made it a real challenge," said the award-winning Plunkett before the luncheon. "It, of all costumes, had to be completely right. Because of this, they [MGM] permitted me to design the outfit first, then they made the draperies to correspond. In other words, the drapes had to be equipped with the proper tie-back cords and tassels to form the trim on the dress.

Strangely enough, few people noticed the hat. If you look closely, you'll see it was trimmed with chicken feathers and gilded chicken feet."

According to the designer, GWTW posed many an unusual problem for those concerned with the costuming.

"Take Scarlett's first wedding dress for example," he said. "This was a hasty wartime marriage. Scarlett's dress was the one that had been worn by her mother. To get the authentic 'taken in' look, we actually made the dress on the dressmaker's form of Barbara O'Neill, who played her mother in the film. The design was also twenty years before the date of the story."

Mr. Plunkett is a quiet, tall, distinguished-looking man, now retired, who started out in Hollywood years ago. He has dressed the world's most beautiful women, and has a designing influence on the lives of such women as Katharine Hepburn, Ava Gardner, Elizabeth Taylor, Lana Turner, Shirley MacLaine, Judy Garland, and Vivien Leigh, to name a few. His designs for GWTW helped make it a masterpiece.

"I read the book twice," he told Stephens Mitchell, brother of the GWTW author, at the luncheon. "The first time, I made notations of every line and passage containing a reference to clothes or related subjects. Your sister was one of the most charming women I've ever met, and she was a great help in introducing me to people working in museums in Charleston, Savannah and here."

Mr. Plunkett has been back to Atlanta only one time since the trip when he worked with Miss Mitchell on the dress designs.

"I came back to the second premiere," he recalled. "I remember going out to a party after the show at the home of Mr. and Mrs. [Alfred] Kennedy. Your First Lady of Georgia was there, and she looked lovely and was wearing one of the gowns I designed for Elizabeth Taylor to wear in *Raintree*

County. As I recall, the picture was here then for a centennial celebration."

The First Lady referred to was Mrs. Ernest Vandiver, and the events were for the Centennial, for which Mrs. Kennedy was the chairman.

At the reunion luncheon, Secretary of State Ben Fortson was one of the honorees. Another guest was British actor Jan Hanson, who played the part of Charles Hamilton, Scarlett's first husband, in the stage version of the book in London. He is now a member of the cast of *As You Like It*, which has just completed a run here. Scarlett and Rhett were there, too. The two wax figures were from the Wax Museum of Underground Atlanta.

This writer, wearing a Coca-Cola bottle-opener necklace, was told by Mr. Plunkett, "Better hold on to that, you can make money on it. I was in an antique shop in Los Angeles recently and there was a wooden case holding twenty-four empty Coke bottles. I know all of us have had those in days gone by, but guess what the price was? One hundred and fifteen dollars. Can you believe it?"

Just before rushing away from the luncheon, to see the Atlanta Historical Society's exhibit at Neiman-Marcus which includes many GWTW items as well as one of his original costume sketches, he said, "One more thing I must tell you about Atlanta. On my first visit here, doing research, I had a call from a woman who said she had saved innumerable hoops and different types of underwear and corsets. These items, believe it or not, were hard to find, even in the most complete museums.

"I finally found the house and rang the doorbell. A woman peeked through the curtains and motioned me to wait. Finally, the door opened and a little old lady, I'm sure she was up in her seventies, apologized. She had had to put her mother in another room in the house and lock the door, all because I was wearing a blue suit. Mother, it seems, thought I was a Yankee and was about to grab her rifle!" (Yankee soldiers wore blue uniforms.)

So, with that, Mr. Plunkett was GWTW himself. And he's probably back now in his beloved California. Now retired, he lives in an apartment overlooking the Pacific. He has been touring Europe in a trailer and stopping to record with oils, on canvas, subjects that interest him.

Dicksie McCutchen's Gone With the Wind Party

June 28, 1971

O F COURSE YOU have heard about *Gone With the Wind,* the book *and* the movie. But what you haven't heard about is the *Gone With the Wind* costume ball debut of Dicksie Linn McCutchen of Dalton [now Mrs. Alec Hill of Atlanta].

On Friday, June 25, 1971, at the Piedmont Driving Club, the ball was given by her parents, Mr. and Mrs. Joseph Kelly McCutchen of Dalton. There hasn't ever been a ball among debutante circles here like this one.

Miss McCutchen is a member of the Phoenix Debutante Group. She had a date for her debut with James Leonidas King III, from Macon, who in the mode of the evening wore a Confederate officer's uniform.

Miss McCutchen may have had a date with "General" King, but there to the left of the receiving line (the honoree, her parents, and her brother, Joe McCutchen, Jr., and his wife from Ellijay) were twenty-six young men wearing styles of 1971—white tuxedo jackets. They were the honorary hosts, according to the real hosts, but it really appeared as though the little blonde debutante had twenty-seven dates for the ball.

The ball began at 9:00 P.M., and at about 9:45 everyone had arrived. The girls all wore antebellum dresses, and their escorts came dressed as Confederate soldiers, party-goers of the sixties, or plantation owners. Nobody dared attend as a Yankee soldier.

The orchestra, a group called Whyrl, started playing "Dixie," and Dicksie McCutchen went whirling onto the dance floor with her father for the first dance. Her brother broke in for a few steps, then her date, and then, as you might expect, her twenty-six honorary escorts broke in and the ball began.

The big ballroom at the club has been decorated for many and varied themes over the years. Friday night it was dressed for *Gone With the Wind.* Nine columns marched down each side of the room, and suspended from each at the ceiling height was a Confederate flag approximately four by six feet in size. A white picket fence entwined with magnolias surrounded the bar set in the alcove; the other bars were draped with flags. Stirring sticks stamped "Dicksie's Debut" were topped with miniature flags, match covers read the same, and a big banner across the entrance proclaimed, you've guessed it, "Dicksie's Debut."

Scarlett O'Hara took a back seat, as it were, because on a huge medallion hanging in the alcove there was a picture of Dicksie gazing at the come-hither eyes of Clark Gable (Rhett Butler) in the other medallion.

Confederate caps with bands reading "Dicksie's Debut" were used as table decorations, and at midnight, with the band playing "Dixie," the caps were thrown among the crowd as favors. If you have ever been to a graduation at West Point or Annapolis, when cadets toss their caps, then you've got the picture.

The debutante wore a red satin antebellum gown. She also wore a diamond heart pendant given her by her parents on her nineteenth birthday last month. She was born on Memorial Day. Are you wondering why a Rebel born on this Yankee Memorial Day doesn't spell her name Dixie? Because Dicksie is a family name.

Members of all three debutante groups (The Atlanta, Phoenix, and Cherokee) and their dates were invited, as were the debutante's ADPi sorority sisters at Emory University, and friends from throughout the state. Watching the ball, with the girls floating past in the hoop skirts and the men looking handsome like the beaux of the sixties, one couldn't help recalling the first *Gone With the Wind* ball here, sponsored by the Junior League in celebration of the premiere of the movie.

The late Tom Ham, one of the many newsmen covering that gala event, wrote, "They draped the hall for auld lang syne with flags of stars and bars, and all the local belles were there, and all their Mas and Pas."

Dicksie's Debut is certainly one for the memory books.

Yolande's Atlanta

Southern Charmers

Important People

August 2, 1943

I'LL BET YOU meet the most interesting people!" is a remark newspaper reporters hear constantly.

It's true, too. We do meet interesting people. We meet them and interview them, and sometimes fine friendships result, and, above all, good and important contacts are made.

But that's not all. We learn people. We learn that the bigger the person, the more human he or she will act. It's only the Mr. Smartypants who has just received a title, or some bootlicking individual who has just become an executive, who is so impressed with himself that he forgets that phrase, "I am a man, and nothing human can be of indifference to me."

These types bore, disgust and amuse. In a way, they are like the old saying, "He was like the cock who thought the sun had risen to hear him crow!" It is far below their position to be human beings. Instead, they are boring, and so obviously trying to impress and to climb.

President Roosevelt happens to have the biggest job in the country. Once while attending a press conference at the White House, I defied White House rules to remain a minute after the conference was over to say hello to FDR. I was a visiting reporter, and when I spoke he said, "Hello, Atlanta, how's everything? And how are Clark and Margaret (Brigadier General and Mrs. Clark Howell)? Give them my best!"

A big man like FDR can be human, not using his position to the point of aloofness, indifference and downright rudeness. A big man is democratic, and is sure of himself and his position. Those who aren't feel unsafe on the pedestal they have finally managed to scale.

Ambassador William Bullitt, stopping over at Candler Field, was meat for a reporter's appetite. Did we stand in the waiting room in formal conversation to get an interview? No. The handsome, bald diplomat said, "Can't we go in here to the fountain and have some coffee and talk? I think we would both enjoy it more." (To say I did, was putting it mildly.)

Vivien (Scarlett O'Hara) Leigh flopped down on a couch in her suite at the Georgian Terrace hotel during the *Gone With the Wind* premiere and asked, "Do you know where I can get a refill for this lipstick?"

Laurence Olivier, then her fiancé, sauntered in, sat down and asked, "Do you people here drink Coca-Cola all the time?"

Clark (Rhett Butler) Gable walked in and said, "I'm nervous about leading the grand march at the Junior League ball with your Miss Margaret Palmer! Leading a grand march is a little out of my line!"

Movie big shots, but were they standoffish trying to be important as do some small fry? They autographed everything except checkbooks.

Opera singer Grace Moore gave an interview while she ate creamed chicken on toast, salad, and hot rolls. She was hungry and admitted it. "I'm always starved at this time of night!" she laughed. Many would have died before letting a reporter see the menu, much less admit their hunger.

[44]

Dorothy Thompson doesn't give one the brushoff as do some self-styled busy and important matrons. Once, in Washington, we searched the corridors of the House Office Building for a newspaper, of all things! "It's this lend-lease bill; I've got to see what the latest developments are." A novice or Mr. Smartypants would not have let me know he didn't know the latest.

Alice Roosevelt Longworth and I exchanged conversation pieces once during a Senate hearing. She later told me, "It was like writing notes in school. Next time I'll bring more paper so we can talk more!"

J. Edgar Hoover, the idol of millions, will invite you into his office in the Justice Building without pomp and ceremony. He is natural. Once he showed me his mother's picture on his desk. A man as big as Hoover could be emotionally brave. A little man would be afraid to appear sentimental.

Admiral William Glassford, now in Dakar for FDR, said during an interview, "Where, on this side of the Atlantic, lady, did you get that red hat?"

A boy named Corrigan, who flew the wrong way to gain fame, whispered during an interview, "Couldn't we slip out of here, and go some place and get a hamburger and some milk?"

There is no red tape or fuss about interviewing Mrs. Roosevelt. She is far easier to talk to than some newly elected officer of a local club!

When Mrs. Hattie Carraway of Arkansas became the first woman senior senator upon the death of her colleague, Senator Joe Robinson, she was unashamed of her tears. She told me outside the Senate chamber, "I know I shouldn't show my feelings like this, but I can't help it." For a newspaper woman's eyes, many women would have controlled themselves to appear "brave."

Colonel Charles Lindbergh, who flew to fame, is openly rude to the press. He doesn't like us and doesn't fail to let us know it. He once told me, "If you are a reporter, I'm busy and haven't time to talk to you!" (It may be just a coincidence, but look what's happened to him now!)

The only person I've ever interviewed bearing a name of importance who was evidently impressed by herself was her Imperial Highness, the Grand Duchess Marie of Russia. She told me, among many things, that she didn't like American men. Being a lady first and a reporter second, I let her rave on, then came into the office and took it out on the city editor, and then told on the Duchess.

I spent many happy and congenial weeks doing editorial work for Mrs. Royal S. Copeland and her late husband, U. S. Senator Copeland, of New York, at the Shoreham Hotel in Washington. It was just like being with home folks.

All reporters don't wear wings, and probably never will; but the little men and little women might remember this, "Be not forgetful to entertain strangers, for thereby some have entertained angels unawares."

Most reporters have X-ray eyes when they meet "these interesting people," and take in a lot they don't print.

The Dorseys Kept Cow, Ponies at Mansion on Peachtree

November 9, 1952

THE QUIET LIFE Mrs. Hugh Dorsey now leads is a far cry from the time she was First Lady of Georgia and lived in the executive mansion at the corner of Peachtree and Cain streets.[1]

"I have a complete, new setup now," said the widow of Georgia's World War I governor, "for since the governor died I have moved from our place farther out and am living in a duplex on 28th Street with my son, Hugh, Jr., and his wife and children.

"I really don't do anything startling or exciting. I have enjoyed traveling a great deal. I spent September at High Hampton and prior to that I was in Cuba. I have not settled myself enough to even unpack some of my things and even haven't gotten around to planning a garden."

Turning back the clock to the time she was First Lady, Mrs. Dorsey, who possessed all the charm, refinement, and background the position should demand, recalled many interesting things. She was the last of the state's First Ladies to live in the old Victorian mansion that stood where the

---

[1] Gov. Hugh Dorsey died in 1948. His wife died July 22, 1966.

Mary Wilkinson Dorsey, First Lady during World War I

Henry Grady Hotel now stands.[2] (Governor Dorsey was succeeded by Thomas Hardwick, who lived at the Georgian Terrace.) Atlanta's builders spearheaded the march of progress which doomed the place for destruction.

"We lived at the mansion during the first World War. Naturally, the times brought more than the usual number of distinguished visitors to our city. We entertained Vice-President and Mrs. Coolidge and General John J. Pershing, to name a few. Of course, Mr. Coolidge was as silent here as everywhere, but Mrs. Coolidge was very talkative and very nice.

"As with everybody in public life, we had little privacy. The mansion's lot extended to Spring Street and was enclosed with an iron fence. I don't find it unusual to hear that a governor keeps a cow at the mansion. We had one, too, and my boys, Hugh and James, had their ponies there.

"I entertained soldiers from Camp Gordon every week at tea parties. Yes, it was tea, because those were prohibition days. There was always a great number who came by. We had official receptions for the Georgia House and Senate.

"They were by invitation only and not the 'open house' type of affair which later was the custom. The legislature met in the summer then. One of the most exciting days I recall was that of the Armistice Day parade. Our yard was jammed with people, and they even sat atop the fence to watch the celebration."

Prominent and popular, the Dorseys kept pace with their contemporaries, with the very young set and friends of their sons, as well as the debutante set. The governor's niece, Mary Faith Yow of Lavonia, came to Atlanta to spend the season at the executive mansion to make her debut with the belles

---

[2] The Henry Grady was razed in 1972; today the Peachtree Plaza Hotel stands on the site.

bowing then. Miss Yow was a member of the 1919 Atlanta Debutante Club, which was headed by Dorothy Haverty (Mrs. Lon Grove). The Dorseys presented their niece to society at a dance at the nearby Capital City Club, which stood on Peachtree near Ellis, where Davison's now stands.

Architect Philip Shutze Designs Beauty

May 11, 1975

WHEN PHILIP TRAMMELL Shutze[1] was a little boy, he loved to draw pictures. They were the usual kind for a child —houses, buildings with square windows, and churches with the steeples a bit off-center.

His uncle, the late Thomas C. Erwin, was an Atlanta banker who used to watch him draw and kept a close eye on his lines and ideas. So one day he told his nephew he was sending him to an architectural school, Georgia Tech.

Today, the drawings of Philip Trammell Shutze have become physical beauty spots on the face of Atlanta as well as stars dotting the map of architectural highlights in Georgia and South Carolina.

His architectural works have won him fame, prizes, and a neat little fortune.

Shutze's artistry is classical, and he terms himself a classicist.

"I really believe that the young architects are changing their viewpoint, and are realizing that some of the old and beautiful work is more attractive and more livable than this

---

[1] Philip Shutze died October 17, 1982.

Phillip Trammell Shutze, architectural classicist and genius

overflow of cold, inhuman-looking buildings. They don't even relate to human beings," said Shutze. "Thank heavens there is a trend to nice things and pretty things. There is one place here that, so help me, looks like Lenin's tomb."

Born in Columbus, Shutze received a Bachelor of Science degree in architecture from Tech and a Bachelor of Architecture degree from Columbia University in New York. He was awarded the Prix de Rome in 1915, and studied as a fellow at the American Academy in Rome, Italy. Mead, of the noted architectural firm of McKim, Mead and White, pronounced his solution to the senior competition the best work by a student ever seen.

The beautiful work he has done bears out his statement. Take the Swan House as an example, right here in Atlanta. It was built by Shutze and his associates in 1928 as the home for the late Mr. and Mrs. Edward Inman. Mrs. Inman was a devoted admirer of William Kent and his colleagues, thence the home and gardens were inspired by the Palladian School of Architecture which flourished in England from the time of Queen Anne through the reign of George II.

The Temple on Peachtree Road and the Academy of Medicine on West Peachtree are two other outstanding examples of his work. He has also done buildings on the Emory University campus such as the Whitehead wing and memorial room, the Walter Rich building, the entrance gates to the campus, and the Glenn Memorial Methodist Church and the Little Chapel.

Among other Shutze buildings spotting the city are C&S banks, the Southern Bell Telephone Company buildings, Sears, Roebuck & Co., and the old Howard Theatre.

In the residential section, in addition to the Swan House, are the Goodrum-Abreau home on West Paces Ferry Road, now owned by Mrs. W. W. Rushton, and the Harry English home, also on West Paces Ferry Road and now the home of Mrs. Anne Cox Chambers.

The home built for the late Mr. and Mrs. William H. Kiser faced on West Paces Ferry Road. Then Knollwood Road was cut through and the estate divided into lots, so the entrance is now on Knollwood. Dr. and Mrs. Bernard Wolff owned it and lived there many years. The next owners were Mrs. Florence Cliff Horton and her son, Gordon Horton.

Other beautiful homes Shutze built for Atlantans were those for Dr. and Mrs. Floyd McRae on Habersham Road, for Mr. and Mrs. Toulman Williams on Garmon Road, and for Mr. and Mrs. Edward Van Winkle, also on Habersham Road; the Paces Ferry Road home of Mr. and Mrs. Ben T. Smith, the M. A. Ferst home on Clifton Road, and the West Paces Ferry Road home built for the late Mr. and Mrs. Andrew Calhoun which is now the home of Mr. and Mrs. Allison Thornwell. Atlantans know it as the Pink Palace.

The Shutze touch is also found in south Georgia and South Carolina. Among those for whom he designed homes are Mr. Julian Hightower of Thomaston and Mrs. Raymond Demere in Savannah, and Albany homes for Mrs. Charles Daniel, Francis Weatherbee, and Mrs. E. S. McKissick. And suppose Shutze ever decided to build and design his own home—he lives in an apartment—what would it be like?

A simple, little, brick Maryland-style home.

"As I think there is a trend toward 'nice' things, I'd follow my own design of thinking and doing," he said.

Two Mrs. Talmadges
Graced the Mansion

June 23, 1974

B EFORE 1968, GEORGIA'S First Families lived in the big Stone Mountain granite mansion on the Prado in Ansley Park. Edwin P. Ansley, developer of Ansley Park, built the big thirteen-room house for his family in the early 1900s. Several other families bought and sold it during the years; until in October, 1924, it was leased, and later bought, as the state's executive mansion. The first occupants were Governor and Mrs. Clifford Walker.

Often called the "royal family of Georgia politics" are the Talmadges,[1] Eugene and his son, Herman. Herman is now Georgia's senior United States senator, who divides his time between Washington and his home in Lovejoy. His mother, Mrs. Eugene Talmadge, widow of the state's sixty-seventh governor and affectionately known as "Miss Mit", lives in her white-columned home in McRae. In an interview there she

---

[1] "Miss Mit" Talmadge died October 20, 1981. Senator Herman Talmadge and his wife, Betty, were divorced in 1977. Mrs. Talmadge maintains the home and farm at Lovejoy, Georgia, where her pig business is still a great success. Senator Talmadge was defeated for re-election in 1980, and currently lives in Lovejoy, Georgia.

The Talmadges: Mattie (Miss Mit) and her husband Eugene

said "Oh, yes, I remember living at the mansion up in Atlanta. I also remember what a hard time we had trying to get rid of all those wild onions on the front lawn."

"We had the driveway paved as soon as we got there, and also had the tennis courts resurfaced. We brought a cow up from the farm (in McRae) and kept her there in the barn, and she grazed in the front yard. We had some nice next-door neighbors, Dr. and Mrs. Herbert Reynolds, and Dr. Reynolds used to love buttermilk, so I'd see that he got a gallon or so each week.

"We kept three saddle horses up there, too. Eugene and I loved to ride, and usually rode early in the morning through the wooded area in Ansley Park. There were a lot of woods in those days. We had a friend, Mrs. Stacey Hill, who liked to ride, and sometimes she would take us out to a stable off Paces Ferry Road to ride the trails out there."

"Miss Mit" said she and the governor didn't go in for so much party-giving except for the official functions. She did say, however, that they would have the family in for meals just as always.

Mrs. Talmadge made nationwide news several times while she was at the mansion. One time the Old Guard party-givers were fascinated when a story appeared in which she was quoted as saying that she was having a reception, but was serving "sho-nuff" sandwiches that men like rather than the little bite-sized, tea-party types.

She takes care of her roses, azaleas, and gardenias nowadays at her McRae home, but she says there are too many pine trees to have much of anything else, except for the farm section. And would she like to be First Lady again?

"No, this is too bad a time to be in politics. And another thing, I don't look back or talk much about what has been. I like to look and think in the future."

Now, there is the other former First Lady, Mrs. Herman

Talmadge, the former Betty Shingler of Ashburn. She and the senator were at their home in Lovejoy recently for a Father's Day celebration with their sons, Eugene and Bobby,[2] and their families.

"I had a real feeling of nostalgia the other day," said Mrs. Talmadge. "Gordon Roberts (Herman's press secretary) was showing me some interior shots of the old mansion. It certainly brought back memories.

"Herman and I were married there. We had planned to marry later in the winter, but he called me and said he had a three-day pass before being shipped to the Pacific. This was during World War II. He said, 'Let's get married now'. I was in Ashburn, and had to rush to Rich's and get some clothes, and we married on Christmas Eve of 1941. Papa Eugene was the best man. He and Mother Talmadge were living at the mansion then. I married in my traveling outfit, as I didn't have a chance to get a wedding dress. My parents, Mr. and Mrs. Simon Shingler, came up with me.

"Herman went on overseas and I stayed with the Talmadges for a while, until Herman came back. Little Gene was born the following year at Piedmont Hospital, and I brought him back to the mansion to spend his early babyhood there.

"I was twenty-four when I became First Lady, and Herman and I first moved into the mansion in 1947. I had my hands full with the children—I had Bobby by then—and, anyway, we were not much on party-giving. Looking back now, I can hardly believe that at twenty-four I held the responsibilities of a First Lady.

"One night Herman came home and announced that he wanted to have members of the state legislature for dinner two nights later. I asked him how many there would be, and

---

[2] Bobby Talmadge drowned in Lake Lanier on May 25, 1975.

Betty and Herman Talmadge later occupied the Governor's mansion

when he said, 'Four hundred,' I almost died! We didn't hire a caterer in those days, so the servants and some friends helped me and we cooked all the next day and night. I called Mr. Yohannan, who was then manager of the Piedmont Driving Club, and borrowed pots and pans and napkins and a few other things. I just didn't have enough to cook for or to serve that many people. I was so pleased that everything was ready; then Herman came home that night and said the dinner had to be postponed. I had to refrigerate the hams and the turkeys, and the rest of the food was used a part of our menu for the next week.

"We were not party-minded, but I do remember when we had an official reception for Adlai Stevenson, when he was running for president and came to Georgia.

"There were no bodyguards or state troopers for Herman and me, and we lived just like any other young married couple. I'll never forget—one night the phone rang and I heard Herman say, 'Why, sure, come right on out. We'll be glad to see you.' I asked who was coming, and he said he didn't know, but a man said he was in town and couldn't get a hotel room and asked if he could spend the night at the mansion. He came, and we gave him the downstairs bedroom. He had breakfast with us the next morning and then left. We found out his name was Henry Surplin, but we didn't know him. I've heard that in politics you have to please everybody, so I suppose that was a good example."

When Herman Talmadge again returned to the mansion as the state's seventy-first governor in 1948, Mrs. Talmadge says Mrs. William T. Healey, a long-time friend of the Talmadge family, was wonderful to her, not only by being a friend, but also by advising her and guiding her through the rough waters of politics.

"We had a caterer then, and entertaining wasn't so hard, but we just gave official functions. Personal entertaining was out of the question and we were not social-minded. I learned that when in politics you have to listen to the right people, and Mrs. Healey was certainly one of those people.

"Yes, I would like to relive some of those years. I enjoyed them. And, yes, I suppose I would like to be Georgia's First Lady again."

She is still a leading lady here in her native state, and on the national scene in Washington she is sought after for many events and campaigns.

Mrs. E. D. Rivers Was
a Gracious Hostess

July 28, 1974

EURITH DICKINSON RIVERS was Georgia's sixty-eighth governor. He and his pretty brunette wife, the former Lucile Lashley, came here from their home in Lakeland, Georgia, to live in the Governor's Mansion in Ansley Park.[1] Rivers became governor in 1937 and served until 1947.

His inauguration day was marked by a parade, a reception at the mansion, and an inaugural ball at the Shrine Mosque. Earlier in the day the formal inauguration ceremony had taken place at the Capitol. Through it all his wife was by his side, just as she had been since they eloped while they were seniors at Young Harris College. They kept the marriage a secret until after their graduation a few days later in June, 1914.

Governor and Mrs. Rivers had two children, E. D., Jr., and Geraldine. The latter is now Mrs. J. J. Mangham, Jr., of Bremen. She was in the city recently for a visit with the family of her daughter, Mrs. Peter Wilcox. While here, Mrs.

---

[1] Governor E. D. Rivers died June 11, 1967. His wife, Lucile, died May 6, 1976.

The Rivers: Lucile Lashley and her husband Eurith Dickinson

Mangham, speaking for her mother, recalled some of the happy days during her late father's term as governor.

Mrs. Rivers was one of the most socially-minded First Ladies of Georgia, and delighted in entertaining at the mansion.

"I had just finished my freshman year at Young Harris College when Dad was elected governor," Mrs. Mangham said. "Politics were very exciting in those days, and vast crowds would attend the speakings of the candidates. Everyone took great interest in the issues, and in the candidates and their families. Those were the days of long motorcades, barbecues, fish fries, pink lemonade, buttons, hats, and car stickers.

"When we moved into the mansion, Mother's first thoughts were of the kitchen. A new stove was badly needed, as well as additional cabinets. The state dining room was the only dining area. Mother wanted a large paneled informal breakfast room because we often had guests for breakfast, as well as lunch and dinner, and many of our friends brought their small children. She continually asked until she got her informal dining area, which proved a real joy for our friends and for us.

"The inaugural receptions, teas and other social functions were all planned by Mother, often with the aid of our good friend, Mrs. Mamie K. Taylor. When Mother was in the receiving line or mingling with guests, Mrs. Taylor's watchful eye saw that everything ran smoothly. She and Mother were superb organizers. Mother planned the week's menu in advance, and the grocery lists were given to the butler or the chauffeur, whichever one was available, to do the shopping."

One of Mrs. Mangham's most cherished possessions is her scrapbook on *Gone With the Wind*.

"One of the highlights of our time at the mansion was the premiere of *Gone With the Wind*. We had a tea at the mansion for the movie stars and the visiting dignitaries, and they were all very gracious and charming. I shall never forget Carole Lombard's complete devotion to Clark Gable. She lost sight of him momentarily, when the large number of people greeting him had separated them. She turned to me and said, 'Oh, where is he? I don't see Clark.' I finally spotted him with a group of people and she said, 'Isn't he wonderful? Oh, I must be close to him!'

"Later, I went into the kitchen. There were Carole and Clark talking to the cook, the butler and the maid. Clark was asking the cook what she was taking out of the oven. When he was told it was cornbread, Clark immediately asked for a piece buttered, and said he much preferred it to the canapés.

"At the premiere Vivien Leigh sat with Mother and Dad, and my husband and I sat behind them. I noticed Miss Leigh crying and my mother comforting her. Later, I asked Mother why she was crying. Mother said she (Miss Leigh) was crying because she was afraid people would be disappointed in her in the movie. Imagine that! Of course, the greatest moment of all came when the matchless Margaret Mitchell was escorted down the aisle by Clark and Carole, at the invitation of Mayor Hartsfield, to stand with the producer, David O. Selznick, and be presented to the audience with other stars from the cast."

Mrs. Mangham said that when President Franklin D. Roosevelt came to Georgia for a visit, it was another highlight of the period, and that of all the dignitaries she met in those days, he was by far the most dynamic, with the most irresistible personality. She said her father was behind him one hundred percent on his national program. It was a very crucial time in Georgia history.

"I know Dad was very grateful to have served at this time," continued Mrs. Mangham. "He was often referred to as Georgia's first modern governor. He was the first with a progressive plan for the 'little man.' His constructive programs are still intact today, and are a living tribute to him. When Dad died, a friend wrote me and said, 'I didn't realize how many wonderful things we enjoy today that we owe to Governor Rivers.'

"Mother contributed much to Dad's career. She taught school and worked long hours in the campaign headquarters when she wasn't on the campaign trail with him. Mother did not make speeches, but she believed in the work Dad was doing. She was his sounding board, and he frequently asked her views on matters. She is candid, courageous and genuine, with a fine sense of humor, and Dad respected her woman's intuition.

"Mother is now a patient at the Seventh Day Adventist Nursing Home in Lakeland. She doesn't speak now, but she communicates by raising a finger to answer, 'yes.' If you were to ask her if she would like to be First Lady again, I rather believe that her blue eyes would twinkle and, smiling, she would lift two fingers to signify, 'yes, yes.' . . . . a very indomitable spirit."

The Music Queen of Atlanta, Margaret Perrin

October 24, 1976

THE ENTERTAINMENT WORLD has its Music Man. But Atlanta, thankfully, has her Music Queen.

She is Margaret Perrin, and people all over town have danced to her peppy music as well as to her dreamy waltzes. They have enjoyed her at parties, where her background music lends that certain something to the incessant cocktail chatter. At fashion shows, like the famous Fashionata by Rich's Sol Kent, the models have that bouncy gait because of her music, and at wedding receptions she almost steals the spotlight from the newlyweds.

Now she has captured another audience—Mexico City, Mexico.

She is back from south of the border after a thrilling trip. She was invited by American ambassador Joseph John Jova to play at a gala cocktail buffet at the U. S. Embassy residence in Lomas.

It was a perfect setting for the Atlantan. The place was jammed with VIPs of the diplomatic, social, business, and fashion worlds. She felt right at home playing for this special event, which was the presentation of the fall-winter collection of designer Liz Claiborne.

[67]

Gov. George Busbee (L) and wife Mary Beth (R) with Margaret Perrin

Last year, for the first time, the Palacio de Hierro recognized an international designer producing his line in Mexico by awarding the gold medal from its Hall of Fame to Oscar de la Renta. This year, the prestigious gold medal was given to Liz Claiborne as an outstanding young international designer producing a line in Mexico.

Margaret Perrin played not only during the cocktail hour, but also during the fashion presentation show.

"Oh, I played the usual type of music I play here at home when we have a fashion show. You know, the light, bubbly numbers from Cole Porter, and Rodgers and Hart, and others, as well as from current Broadway shows. I had two Mexican musicians, a bass player and a drummer, accompany me at the party.

[68]

"The clothes presented were beautiful. I met many leading Mexicans, and all in all it was one of the most exciting things that has ever happened to me. The people down there were just charming."

Going with her to Mexico City were the ambassador's brother, well-known Atlanta architect, Henri Jova, along with Jinx Drake, Dr. Olin Shivers, and David Rinehart.

The Atlanta keyboard artist is still enjoying a fabulous career. She and her brother, Forrest, were a popular piano team, appearing on WSB's Kiddie Club. They played for years at Club 21 in New York, once had a "Piano Playhouse" show on radio, and were selected as one of the ten most popular programs among servicemen overseas during World War II. On the invitation of the government, they went overseas to entertain the servicemen. Once they played in Germany on a stage formed by two Army trucks backed together. One of the pianos had been out in the rain all night, but they managed to get the show on the road like all professionals. During one show in North Africa, the majority of the soldier-audience was French. So, what did the team do? They played French songs.

When they returned to the States, they received citations of merit from the government.

Forrest Perrin is still in New York, playing like crazy. Margaret is back home with a date book filled for "playing" all over town.

She plays during the weekend at the Piedmont Driving Club, and when the debutantes are presented, it's Margaret and her band right there playing for the presentation.

A band? "Oh, yes, I have a band. For most home cocktail parties I just play solo. I only have men musicians in the band. We get along just fine, and they don't seem to mind that they have a woman as their boss," she says.

She helped organize the Cracker Crumble, an annual

political satire sponsored by the Georgia Press Association. She's a great favorite for society balls, here and in other sections of the South. And in a situation similar to her recent trip to Mexico to play for the gala fashion affair, she was tapped by fashion leaders in New York to come there to play when the Coty awards were made.

Most impressively, she seldom uses the music sheet. Her terrific talent is all right there in her ten fingers.[1]

---

[1] Margaret Perrin still lives in Atlanta.

Mrs. Ellis Arnall Saw History Made

July 7, 1974

WHEN ELLIS ARNALL was elected Georgia's sixty-ninth governor, he and his pretty wife, Mildred, and a very frisky five-year-old son, Alvan, piled into the family car and headed for Atlanta where they were to spend the next four years.

Their small comfortable home in Newnan, with its one bathroom, seemed a long way from their "new home," with its five bathrooms, atop an elevated lot in Ansley Park. This was the state's executive mansion on the Prado, a street originally called the Prater after the avenue in Vienna which it reputedly resembled.

As soon as the Arnalls were settled in the thirteen-room mansion, things began to happen. In fact, during the entire Arnall regime from 1943 to 1947, there were happenings almost around the clock.

"As soon as we arrived," said Mrs. Arnall[1] in her home in Newnan, "I enrolled Alvan in the Fritz Orr Camp and the

---

[1] Mrs. Arnall died June 29, 1980, after a heart attack. Former Governor Arnall married Ruby McCord on July 15, 1981. The Arnalls live in Newnan, Georgia. His law office is in Atlanta.

Mildred and Ellis Arnall hosted many dignitaries at the mansion

Spring Street School. From almost the day we arrived until we moved back home, visitors came calling. I shall never forget the political greats who came from throughout the nation. One of the first big parties I gave was for the vice-president of the United States, who was, at that time, Henry A. Wallace. Two of the many famous people who were our guests were Drew Pearson, the columnist, and John Gunther, the author."

It should be noted here that when Arnall was the governor of Georgia, he made many reforms which plunged not only the state but also the Arnalls into the national spotlight. Because of these, a steady stream of writers and members of the news media beat a path to the mansion doors.

What were the reasons? The former governor had the voting age limit lowered to eighteen years. Legislation was also passed to allow blacks to vote in the Democratic primary for the first time, and to abolish the poll tax. Arnall's sensational freight-rate case went before the United States Supreme Court, resulting in a victory for Georgia and the South and giving our state an economic jab in the arm.

Mrs. Arnall said, "We did entertain a great deal, not only for political gatherings, but for a number of good friends who lived in Atlanta. We always had a family party at Christmas, with members coming up from Newnan as well as some of my family from Florida. We gave Halloween parties the last two years we were there, with all Alvan's classmates attending from Spring Street School. We also had some Easter-egg hunts. The big reindeer team running across the mansion roof was put there while we were there, and we had a number of other outside decorations."

Mrs. Arnall said she always planned her menus, although she had a fine cook and a butler. She said, "I think what the Governor's Mansion needs most of all is a good housekeeper. There is a tremendous amount of work involved in running a house that large. I did have good help for the garden at the rear of the mansion. Mr. Monroe did a lot of the planning as well as the planting around the mansion. I had a garden in Newnan, and always loved flowers, fresh ones, in the house."

A state trooper was on duty at all times at the mansion. Mrs. Arnall always drove her own car in Newnan, and when she came here she just kept on driving.

"Living at the mansion was a delightful experience. When we arrived there to begin our term as the First Family, I had planned to spend the first few weeks getting things all straightened up and ready for the company I knew we would have, even for overnight guests like Vice-President Wallace. But all my planning was unnecessary. Miss Mit (Mrs. Eugene Talmadge, who peceded Mrs. Arnall as First Lady) left the place spotless. Everything was in perfect order and ready for us. We could have had a dinner party the night we arrived, if we had wanted to. Miss Mit was, and still is, a superb housekeeper." [1]

Perhaps the most important thing that happened to the First Family while at the mansion was the birth of their daughter, Alice. Alice Arnall has her own place in Georgia history, along with her parents. She is the first and only baby born at the executive mansion. She is now Mrs. Ted Harty and has a three-month-old son.

"We had a fine nurse for her," recalled Mrs. Arnall, "and we had one of the downstairs bedrooms converted into a nursery. Many of our friends called her the Royal Princess, and, of course, to Ellis and myself she was more than that—she was a real jewel."

Aside from this important event in her life and all the other events marking her term as First Lady, would Mrs. Arnall like that title again?

"I enjoyed being First Lady, but I don't think I would like the role again."

---

[1] Miss Mit died on October 20, 1981.

Mrs. Ernest Vandiver Is Still a Charmer

August 4, 1974

FORMER GOVERNOR and Mrs. Ernest Vandiver, Jr.,
live in a beautiful white-columned mansion in Lavonia
which was built by Dr. Ben Yow in 1895. The Vandivers
bought the place, plus a great number of the heavy mahogany
furnishings, from the Yow estate in 1951. It is named Twin
Hollies, and offers this interesting sidelight: one of the Yow
daughters, Mary Faith, spent a winter in Atlanta with her
uncle and aunt, Governor and Mrs. Hugh Dorsey, at the
mansion on the southwest corner of Peachtree and Cain
streets.

Governor and Mrs. Vandiver lived at the executive
mansion in Ansley Park during his term, 1959 to 1963. The
mansion was very familiar to both. Mrs. Vandiver, the
former Betty Russell of Winder, had often been a guest there
while her uncle, the late U. S. Senator Richard Russell, lived
there as the governor. Her late father, Judge Robert Russell,
was a frequent guest there, too. Her husband himself had
served as lieutenant governor under Governor Marvin
Griffin, and before and after these elective offices, he served
as state adjutant general. So visits to the mansion, for him
and his wife, had become almost around the clock.

The Vandivers: Betty and her husband Ernest, Jr.

"The children, Chip (Ernest Vandiver III), now law assistant to Judge Robert H. Jordan on the Georgia Supreme Court), Beth (a case worker with the Family and Children's Services in Athens), and Jane (now Mrs. David Kidd and attending the University of Georgia), were all small," said Mrs. Vandiver at her home.

"I drove them to school at Spring Street every morning. In fact, I was in a car pool for Ansley Park. They could have walked, but I was afraid for them to cross Peachtree Street, and I didn't want them to be driven in a state trooper's car."

Mrs. Vandiver probably has more compassion than any of the other First Ladies of our state. Her love of people and her deep understanding of the needs of others have added jewels to her crown. A case in point was her untiring work for the patients at Milledgeville State Hospital. She spearheaded the drive for the Chapel of All Faiths there. "It was rewarding work," she said. "And now all seminaries require students to take one quarter of work there in psychiatric counseling. Since we opened the chapel, we now have from twelve to fifteen chaplains there at all times. One of the happiest moments I remember was the Christmas we took the thousands of Christmas presents to the hospital. Remember the M Day? Mayors from all over the state cooperated with me.

"We didn't do too much entertaining at the mansion, but had the usual official functions, and, of course, I had the birthday parties for the children. We adhered to a strict economy program." Mrs. Vandiver, however, made plenty of news. She headed the Mothers' March of Dimes in 1954. In 1963 she was named Atlanta's Woman of the Year in Civic Service, in recognition of her outstanding contributions to the Milledgeville State Hospital, and she became the first recipient of the Georgia Chiropractic Association's annual Humanitarian Award.

When the Vandivers did entertain at the mansion, their hospitality was unmatched. "I really loved every minute there, and it was a fine old house. We changed one room so that the two girls could share it. I remember that when we had the inaugural reception there were ten thousand there," said Mrs. Vandiver. "I had to have ten butlers for that party."

Now, back in their home in Lavonia, the Vandivers lead an active but quiet life. They play golf and bridge, and Mrs. Vandiver's needlepoint is everywhere in the home. A pair of pillows in the living room displays on a cream background an original design by Mrs. Vandiver—a spray of holly to depict the name of the big house.

A handsome oil painting by the late Wilbur Kurtz features Georgia's first executive mansion in Milledgeville. Mrs.

Vandiver had a duplicate made as a gift for President Johnson. Her husband took it along with him to give to Johnson when he, J. B. Fuqua, the late Richard Russell, the late Bob Russell, and Carl Sanders went to visit at the LBJ Ranch.

Right now in Vandiver's study at his Lavonia home is a mounted elk head as a trophy of the trip.

In the family den there is a large brick fireplace which the Vandivers had rebuilt when they bought the house. The center brick came from Patrick Henry's home in Virginia and was a gift to them from a relative. On the hearth there is a large flat stone which was part of the headstone on the grave of Vandiver's grandfather five generations back, who was killed in the Revolutionary War. Part of Mrs. Vandiver's bell collection is on the mantel.

When the Vandivers bought the home, they added a large screened porch. It has a ceiling fan acquired when the old Piedmont Hotel was torn down. The spacious home has six outside doors. A winding drive bordered with old boxwood encircles the house, which sits far back from Westwood Drive.

One of Mrs. Vandiver's special collections is her charm bracelets. She has six. One includes all the keys and medals awarded her husband by honor societies, fraternities, etc. She has a birthday one, filled with charms, given her by her husband and children through the years. Her "trip" charm bracelet began when she went to the governors' conference in Montana. She has one from South America and another from Hawaii, and her latest one is from Europe. Each charm is unusual, such as a tiny slot machine, a cuckoo clock, a windmill, a pearl from Pearl Harbor, a diamond from Diamond Head, and a 1925 fifty-cent piece commemorating Stone Mountain, which is rare.

Her charms are not confined to her bracelets. She is one of the charmers of the state, pretty, with dark hair and dark eyes. Would she like to be First Lady again?

"I am so happy here, I never want to leave; but I think I would enjoy reliving some of the happier moments at the mansion."[1]

---

[1]The Vandivers still live in their home in Lavonia, Georgia.

Edwina Garland Merritt Keeps Social History

October 29, 1972

A TLANTA'S SOCIAL HISTORY, pictorially speaking, has been compiled since 1945 by Mrs. Edwina Garland Merritt.

This priceless collection of the city's happenings on the social front should be in a vault instead of in the big, bulging scrapbooks. Better still, it should be at the Atlanta Historical Society. But it isn't complete, for Mrs. Merritt adds something almost every day.

Edwina, as she is fondly known by every woman who has ever been to the Capital City Club, and also by as many men, is the club's popular "hostess with the mostest" in the ladies' lounge at the downtown club. She is on hand for all the big parties at the club, and has never yet given the wrong fur or coat to a guest.

The remarkable thing about Edwina is that she knows everybody by name, and there isn't a woman there who doesn't feel that Edwina is in the lounge for her own special needs. She is a one-woman hospitality committee.

Here is the background on her scrapbooks:

"One afternoon back in 1948, I saw a picture of Mrs. Alvin Cates, Jr., in the paper. I know her, and she looked so pretty

Edwina Garland Merritt has scrapbooks full of memories

in a hat trimmed in camellias. I decided to cut it out," said Edwina. "I had been cutting out pictures and stories of people who came to the club soon after I started working here. I was like everybody—I would stick them away some place, like in my desk or in envelopes. When I saw the big picture of Mrs. Cates, all in color, I decided I would buy a big scrapbook and start pasting in the pictures and the clippings.

"There was so much going on that I found myself clipping the papers almost every day. Look here at these pictures that were used for the Easter parade in 1948. See, there is Mrs. Rankin Smith, with her long hair and that suit with the long jacket, and there is Miss Ellie (Mrs. E. Morgan Montgomery), in that long skirt and a white jacket, and a hat trimmed with a rose. And that is Mrs. Paul Duke over there, and it says she is wearing a gray outfit."

The caption on these pictures said, "A Fifth Avenue Look on Peachtree."

Then there was a picture of Mrs. Bolling Jones examining a wrought-iron table to be copied, and there during the 1949 era was a picture of Mrs. Don Warren of Memphis, Tennessee, the former Rebecca Ashcraft of this city, strolling along with Mrs. William Huger; Mrs. William Healey, Jr.; and Mrs. Henry Tompkins.

A picture captioned "European Tourists" shows Carol Equen (Mrs. Sebastian Miller), Laura Hoppe (Mrs. Bruce Mylrea), and Martha Davis (Mrs. Waddell Barnes), strolling along the Via Veneto in Rome in 1948.

A picture of the 1949-1950 Atlanta Debutante Club is a real shocker, at least by today's standard of dress. The girls were lined up like old-time graduation pictures and all wore ankle-length dresses and hats. There is a similar picture of the new members of the Junior League that year.

A Father's Day feature in 1950 shows the late Ivan Allen

with his son, former Mayor Ivan Allen, Jr., and his two sons, Ivan III and Inman.

And two youngsters shown down on their tummies looking at the comics are Julian Carr, Jr., and Alfred Kennedy, Jr.

Another clipping is the marriage write-up of Janet Appleby to Roy Dorsey in 1948; the bride carried a prayer book topped with a white hyacinth. In the 1949 wedding of Martha Mann and Mark Pentecost, Jr., it was noted that the bride wore her debut dress as her wedding gown. The marriage of Betty Fitts and Neal Irby in 1947 is also in the book.

There is a write-up of the 1950 marriage of Beverly Dobbs and John Mitchell (Edwina was on hand at the reception held at the club) and there is a full-length picture of Sally Prescott and Clayton Rich leaving All Saints Episcopal Church after their marriage in 1949. Other clippings and pictures show Mrs. Oliver Healey as the best-dressed woman of the year for 1947; a 1948 grandmother, Mrs. Lon Grove, with her grandson, Claiborne Glover III; and the wedding write-up of Joan Lang and Dixon Allen.

For years the Capital City Club was the scene of the supper dance following the first-night performance of the Metropolitan Opera. Pictures covering these events are interesting entries. One is former Atlantan Wright Bryan dancing with opera star Bedu Sayao at the 1949 party. And Mrs. Harold Cooledge is noted at the table with the club president, the late George Biggers; and also Charles Jagels with his daughter, Nancy, and John Brownlee.

Atlanta's Woman of the Year in Professions for 1948 was Mrs. Allen Lockerman. Mrs. J. J. Williamson feeding her young son, Jimmy, orange juice, and Mrs. James Porter, Mrs. Perry Ballard, and Mrs. Ed Smith planning a flower show are interesting tidbits for the year.

Another picture that same year shows Mr. and Mrs. Jesse
Shelton at Palm Beach with Mr. and Mrs. L. W. ("Chip")
Robert, Jr.; and also Mrs. Hughes Spalding; her daughter,
Mrs. J. Wallace Winborne, Jr.; and Mrs. Stuart Witham on
a winter visit to Florida. There is a picture of an "Attractive
Newcomer," Mrs. John Wilson, the former Jean Creekmore
of Athens, arranging flowers for her dining room table.
Another picture shows Mrs. Arthur Pew, Jr., cooking
barbecue in a feature called "Meet the Wife." A 1949 Opera
Guild item shows Mrs. Green Warren; Mrs. Ed Chapman,
Jr.; and Mrs. Ed Van Winkle planning a luncheon.

During a rehearsal session for the Tallulah Falls Follies of
1949, some of the highsteppers in a picture include Mrs.
John Cherry; Ann Weyman (Mrs. Cecil Brownlow); Nancy
Jagels; Nancy Keeler (Mrs. Ralph Rhodes); Mrs. Felix de
Golian, Jr.; Mrs. A. G. Cleveland, Jr.; Mrs. Morgan Lewis;
and Florence Northington.

The 1949 *Journal-Constitution Sunday Magazine* sections
carried cover pictures in color of Annette Livingston (Mrs.
Dan Sage, Jr.) in a Red Cross uniform on March 13, and Mrs.
Henry Powell, Jr., and Gwyneth Oliver (Mrs. Wesley
Moran, Jr.) on other dates.

Parties at the club always made special news, and Mrs.
George Woodruff is shown at a holiday event given in 1950.
Also that year, Charles Black and his daughter, Dodo, won
the Labor Day invitational golf tournament.

There are pictures of Mr. and Mrs. Jack Adair leaving the
Cathedral of St. Philip after their marriage; Walter Zillessen,
Jr., kissing his bride after their marriage; Jack Spalding and
Anne Gowen leaving the church at St. Simons after their
marriage.

A full page in 1950 carried a picture of Lindsey Blair and
Bobby Ison, children of Mr. and Mrs. Robert Ison, looking
for Easter eggs. Other 1950 items show Mrs. Sam Inman

[84]

with her young son, Edward, posing in his crib; Mrs. Berrien Moore, Jr., then president of the Junior League, with her children, Jan, Berrien III, and Jody, off to Sunday school; and Mrs. Robert Watt making arrangements for a Woman of the Year dinner.

Mr. and Mrs. James V. Carmichael with two of their children, James, Jr., and Mary Emma, are shown at a club party during opera season in 1955. Back a few years, in 1953, there is a picture of a "Glamorous Grandmother," Mrs. John Knox, with her grandchildren, John O. Knox, Taylor Burgess, and Laura Margaret Burgess (Mrs. Charles E. Hurst, Jr.).

Entered in the book is a decorating feature on the home of Mr. and Mrs. Wilbur Glenn in 1967, and a story on the 1952 New Year's Eve party given at the Peachtree Racket Club.

Other pictures show Mrs. McKee Nunnally dancing with Jackson Dick; and Mr. and Mrs. John Westmoreland, Jr., on the golf links at the country club.

The Westminster School golfers of 1961, Bill Tift, Henry Tift, Morton Hodgson, and Peter Channin, are pictured, and a 1969 cover from the *Journal-Constitution Sunday Magazine* shows Robert Woodruff in hunting togs.

The aforementioned are just a few from the multitude of stories included in Edwina's books.

"I'm still clipping," she said at the club. "In addition to the pictures, I have a lot of news items about the people I know at the club. I'm going to start another book just before Christmas."

Although her primary domain is in the Mirador Room lounge, partygoers know she will be on hand anywhere at the club a party is being given. She is a member of the Ebenezer Baptist Church and has one son, Garland. Her zest for living and her personality could well be linked to the Optimist Creed which she has pasted on the first page of her first

[85]

scrapbook. It ends like this: "To wear a cheerful countenance at all times and give every creature you meet a smile; to give so much time to improvement of yourself that you have no time to criticize others; to be too large for worry, too noble for anger, too strong for fear, and too happy to permit the presence of trouble." [1]

[1]Ms. Merritt still works at the Capital City Club.

Mrs. Carl Sanders Saw World Change

June 30, 1974

WHEN MRS. CARL SANDERS became Georgia's First Lady in 1963, she was, in a manner of speaking, occupying a front-row seat for some of the most dramatic events of this century. Her husband was Georgia's seventy-fourth governor.

"I first remember shedding a few tears when I left my neat three-bedroom, brick house in Augusta to head to Atlanta with my two small children, in the fourth and fifth grades," she said recently while vacationing at her beach house at Sea Island. "We would be living the next four years in a big, drab, gray stone house that sat on the highest hill in Fulton County. As fate would play it, I would learn to love this home, to pamper it, and to find in its awkward rooms a challenge to my homemaking talents."

During their residence at the mansion, the Governor and the First Lady were to suffer the first national shock of violence in their lifetime.

"Our friend, President Kennedy, was assassinated," said Mrs. Sanders. "This was a fast-moving period in my life. I had never dreamed I would some day see my husband become governor of our great state, go through the emotional strain

Betty Sanders saw the world change while she was First Lady

of attending our president's funeral, campaign for a new president and attend his inauguration, and then endure the assassination of Dr. Martin Luther King, Jr., all in four years.

"I guess each woman who graces that home as the state's number one hostess has her own way of doing things. Personally, I liked doing 'my own thing,' as today's generation puts it. When I entertained, it was carefully thought through, especially my legislative dinners, which focused on a theme and featured a matching hand-drawn invitation with verses. These verses were usually written by Naomi Barnard, wife of Doug Barnard, who was Carl's executive secretary."

One of the big parties Mrs. Sanders recalls was the tea she gave at the mansion for First Lady Mrs. Lyndon Johnson, on one of her visits here.

"It was what so many women call a 'peach of a party.' There were about eight hundred guests, and I had big, towering arrangements of ripe peaches in silver epergnes, and massive displays of peach- and cream-toned flowers, and a special peach punch. The chef, Ben Cruz, and I made a special cookie recipe for the event which consisted of chopped, dried peaches and nuts. This became one of my favorite refreshments for later parties for the ladies."

The Christmas cards Governor and Mrs. Sanders sent out in 1964 are now collectors' items. Mrs. Sanders said, "My Christmas cards were another hobby. I asked three of the state's leading art departments to select a student drawing of historical interest in our state. A beautiful and unusual side view of the state capitol was the first, and the old state capitol at Milledgeville was next. The next one made national headlines.

"It was a sketch of the Governor's Mansion on the Prado. It came out the Christmas after we had campaigned hard for the

Democratic nominee, President Lyndon Johnson. As students have a sense of humor at this particular stage in life, this student sketched the word 'Goldwater' in the drawing, almost invisible to the naked eye. Lamar Dodd, head of the University of Georgia Art Department, did not see it, I didn't see it, and it went to press.

"I sent Mr. Ben Fortson one of the first-run prints. One of the secretaries saw the joke. I was jolted. Carl laughed about it, and Lamar Dodd was very upset. I must say I was delighted we chose the subject because, to my knowledge, it is the only drawing of the old house which was the home of the governor for nearly fifty years." (It has since been torn down.)

The last card Governor and Mrs. Sanders sent out was painted by the First Lady herself. It was a composite of governors' homes, including Oglethorpe's tent at Savannah; the first mansion Georgia ever built for a governor, in Milledgeville; the quaint, Gothic Victorian-style mansion on Peachtree where the old Henry Grady Hotel stood (now the site of the Peachtree Plaza Hotel); the Prado mansion; and the new Executive Center. This painting now hangs in the state's Archives Building.

"I was delighted that the new mansion was to be built during my husband's term. The architect, Tom Bradbury, and I had many dining-room conversations about this undertaking. We did extensive study and travel. It was carefully planned and executed by a select group of Georgians, known for their taste, who served as the Mansion Committee. Henry Green, a great authority on Georgia antiques, was chairman and I was co-chairman."

As a gift to the state, Mrs. Sanders wanted to provide the mansion with a large, white marble fountain on the front lawn. A collection of her paintings called "Portrait of

Georgia" toured ten cities to raise the money. Dimes to dollars poured into the little fountain replica, as interested people came to view the paintings. The twenty-foot-round fountain carved with the Greek Key pattern to match the house is a great tribute and monument to Mrs. Sanders.

Looking back, Mrs. Sanders said, "No, I do not have any desire to be First Lady again, but I am eternally grateful to the people who gave me that opportunity. I know Carl and I will always think of things we wish we could have contributed to the state, toward the betterment of all citizens.

"I miss seeing people all over the state—the legislature, the civic clubs and the mill workers who create—but I have treasured the last four years. I have had time to do things after twenty-seven years of marriage and fifteen years of politics that I never before had time to do. One of those things is staying at home. I enjoy my family, too. My son, Carl, Jr., is twenty, and our daughter, Betty Foy, is twenty-two. But I do have a personal project. It's the Betty Foy Sanders Collection of Georgia Artists. I contribute a painting or an art object to the Foy Fine Arts Building, named for my father, at Georgia Southern College in my home town of Statesboro. I have contributed paintings by Ouida Canaday, Joseph Perrin, Lamar Dodd and Wilbur Kurtz, and pottery by Charles Counts. Everyone has something to contribute to life—each in his or her own way."

Mrs. Sanders points with pride to her husband's record in office when he made the Georgia child the star in his administration. Colleges and junior colleges sprang up all over the state and the state's national school rating climbed away from the bottom five or six notches.

A tall, striking beauty, the former First Lady was noted for her hats and was given an award by the Millinery Institute of

America. She also was Cancer Crusade chairman for three years and an honorary chairman of the Atlanta Arts Association, and she did her part in helping women build the Atlanta Memorial Arts Center.[1]

---

[1]The Sanders still live in Atlanta, where the former governor practices law.

Mrs. Lester Maddox Enjoyed Every Minute

July 14, 1974

WHEN MRS. LESTER MADDOX was the First Lady of Georgia, she lived through some very interesting—and sometimes very exciting—times. And there were several "firsts" marking the period from 1967 to 1971.

Her husband was the state's seventy-fifth governor and is now serving as the lieutenant governor.

Mr. and Mrs. Maddox were the first family to live in two executive mansions. Their daughter was the first bride in the new mansion and they, of course, were the first to live in the new mansion on West Paces Ferry Road, often referred to as the Executive Center for the state.

Mrs. Maddox was the first First Lady to stand at the mansion's front door and personally greet the thousands of visitors who came a-calling during the newly instituted open house at the mansion, Monday through Friday from ten o'clock to noon and Sunday from three o'clock to five o'clock.

"The new mansion was not completed when my husband became governor," she said at her home in Marietta recently. "We lived for one year in the old mansion in Ansley Park. We had our first open house there, and I shall never forget it. We were standing in line meeting everybody—and there were

Virginia and Lester Maddox opened the mansion to the public

thousands—when two men who were in the line announced that they were suspects and wanted to turn themselves in to the governor! It frightened me so, I didn't ask them what they meant, and Lester called one of the guards and had them taken away.

"The first dinner we had for the General Assembly was held at a hotel, because the mansion was just not large enough to take care of all of them. I did have small groups and teas there." The former governor and his family moved into the big Greek Revival mansion on West Paces Ferry Road before it was completed.

"Oh, it was livable—I don't mean that," said Mrs. Maddox, "but there were still some interior jobs that had to be done. I'll never forget how one morning when I was dressing, the elevator doors to my bedroom opened up and four workmen came walking into the room to do some work.

"We did have the General Assembly party at the new mansion that year. The beautiful room downstairs, which can be used as a ballroom, too, was a perfect place. While I was there I entertained many different groups, like the senior citizens and the handicapped, and also held a charity fashion show with hundreds attending.

"When we were to move into the old mansion, everybody told us to remember when it rained to run get every pan we could, because the roof leaked. Never once did I notice any leaking. It was a lovely old home, and seemed much more like a private home than the new mansion with all its stateliness and handsome furnishings, but I did enjoy it.

"It takes a heap of living to make a house a home, as the old saying goes, and we tried to do just that. I have always liked to cook, and with that wonderful kitchen there, there is just no way of telling how many dozens of biscuits I have baked. My children love chicken and dumplings, and I have made tons of that, too."

Mrs. Maddox has written a fine and detailed description of the new mansion, which sits on an eighteen-acre tract and which cost the state $2.5 million. It is published in a book entitled *Executive Mansions and Capitols of America* by Jean Houston Daniel and Price Daniel; he was governor of Texas 1959-1963 and she is a great-great-granddaughter of the famous General Sam Houston for whom the city is named.

Virginia Louise Maddox, daughter of the former governor and the First Lady, is the first woman to be married in the present mansion. She became the bride of George Creighton Carnes on November 20, 1970, at a ceremony held in the state drawing room and followed by a reception.

Mrs. Maddox is the former Virginia Cox, who was born in Birmingham, Alabama, but moved to Austell with her parents at an early age.

For a person who had never been in the limelight, especially the political limelight, she is poised and dignified and has a quiet, soft manner which has charmed the thousands who have visited the mansion and whom she has met on various trips. Her garden club, Nancy Creek, wanted to honor its most distinguished member in some way, perhaps with a piece of silver for the mansion. Mrs. Maddox was consulted, and it was her wish that something be done in her name at one of the state's mental institutions, an area of special interest to her.

The result was that the recreation room at the Georgia Retardation Center on North Peachtree Road in Chamblee was furnished in her honor.

"I think one of the most exciting events while I was the First Lady was attending the banquet in Los Angeles honoring the Apollo 11 spacemen. It was the opportunity of a lifetime. It was held at the Century Plaza Hotel, and we were at table seven in the ballroom. The others at the table were scientists and officials connected with the space program. It was absolutely thrilling.

"Another thing I remember was going to dinner at the White House and sitting with 'the O'Briens.' On one side was the actor and TV star Hugh O'Brian and on the other the postmaster general, Lawrence O'Brien."

Before the name of Martha Mitchell became a household word, Mrs. Maddox recalls being seated at the same table with her during a visit to Washington.

"She was the wife of Attorney General John Mitchell, and I didn't think much about it at the time. She was very pretty, had a great personality, and really ran the show at our table."

Mrs. Maddox says she enjoyed having then Vice-President Hubert Humphrey as a guest at the old mansion and Alabama Governor George Wallace at the new one.

"I think what I enjoyed about living at the new mansion was meeting and greeting the thousands of people who came from all over Georgia as well as the country and the world. There were some twenty-five hundred a week, and I personally wanted to greet them and thank them for coming. There were visitors from every state as well as from Europe, Australia, Japan and the Philippine Islands. I kept four scrapbooks the entire time I was at the mansion. I really loved the place."

In addition to the daughter, Mrs. Carnes, the other Maddox children are a daughter, Linda, who is now Mrs. Donald Densmore, and two sons, Lester, Jr., and Larry. And now Mrs. Maddox answers the big question, "Would you like to be First Lady again?"

"Yes, I really would. I enjoyed every minute of it. I would love the second go-round." [1]

---

[1]Mr. and Mrs. Lester Maddox now live in Marietta, Georgia, and Mr. Maddox maintains a real estate business carrying his name.

Mrs. Jimmy Carter Kept Family Close in Mansion

August 11, 1974

MRS. JIMMY CARTER has just a little over four months left to reign as Georgia's First Lady.

This is election year, and a new First Family will be moving into the mansion on West Paces Ferry Road.

"I am looking forward to going back home to Plains," said Mrs. Carter. "I have been going back a great deal lately to get the house ready for us. I always enjoy fixing up things, and the last time I was home I did some painting in one of our four bedrooms.

"I have enjoyed very much my role as First Lady and living in this beautiful mansion. I'll admit that when we moved into this big place it seemed overwhelming, and I was not aware that the duties of a First Lady were so far-reaching. But I certainly realized what I had known always, that no matter what you do, people are always ready to help you. People have been wonderful to me. The time I have lived here I have found most gratifying, and many exciting things have happened."

Mrs. Carter, the former Rosalynn Smith of Plains, has stressed "togetherness" with her family since being in the mansion. As she said when she was getting ready to move in,

Rosalynn and Jimmy Carter made life at the mansion homey

"The mansion will really be used as our home as well as a place for all Georgians to come to visit." But aside from her family duties—four children, including one of kindergarten age—the pretty, brunette wife of the governor has done more than her share in maintaining her home. She has enlarged to a state-wide scale the system of selecting volunteer hostesses for the mansion's open houses, and has been a leader, along with the Garden Club of Georgia and Steve Polk of the state Building Authority, in restoring the mansion's garden terraces to their former beauty and glory. The gardens were once among the beauty spots of Atlanta, situated on the estate of the late former banker and mayor of Atlanta, Robert F. Maddox and Mrs. Maddox; the site of the Maddox home is where the mansion now stands.

Funds for this garden restoration are coming from the sale of a beautiful booklet on the mansion giving its background and a description of its furnishings. It is a very valuable book for those interested in restoration and fine furnishings.

"The book has been quite a favorite, especially for visitors," said Mrs. Carter. "The background on all the furnishings was done by Kitty Farnham and Henry Green, both of whom are authorities. It is paperback, but I had some done with leather backs to give to all the district hostesses as Christmas presents last year."

Mrs. Carter, like another First Lady, Mrs. Ernest Vandiver, has done outstanding work for mental health in Georgia. She says she has toured hospitals, not to find fault, but out of interest and the urge to help. Through her work as a member of the Governor's Commission, the mentally and emotionally handicapped have, in many cases, been moved from these institutions into community centers. Where there were once just twenty-three of these community centers, there are now one hundred and thirty.

Roadside beautification is another interest of Mrs. Carter's. She went to visit Lady Bird Johnson at the LBJ Ranch, along with Georgia garden-club leaders, to gather ideas for use in Georgia from Lady Bird's similar project in Texas.

"I have always loved flowers," said Mrs. Carter, "but since I have been in the mansion, I took a course in flower arranging and try to use fresh flowers all the time. It is certainly cheaper, because we have a greenhouse here as well as a cutting garden. A convention of flower growers came to Atlanta, and, as a part of their visit, they came to tour the mansion on our visitors' day. One man from New York sent me a hundred and twenty rose bushes when he returned, along with a thank-you note. I have the bushes in the cutting garden. One time some visitors were here, and a man from the West, having heard that Jimmy was a peanut farmer, asked if he could see some of the peanut trees! After that, I decided I'd plant some peanuts as a border around one of the flower beds. You know peanuts grow under ground, but have running vines above ground."

On election night when her husband was acclaimed governor, Don Sands of the Goldkist Peanut Company gave Mrs. Carter a small gold peanut lapel pin which she wears all the time.

"There have been numerous prominent guests at the mansion. I remember one time Oral Roberts and his wife came by and had dinner with us. Later, the four of us sat around the counter in the kitchen and talked until about three the next morning. As I said, we made the mansion just as homey as possible. Oh, yes, Billy Graham was our guest, and there was a large party given for Mrs. Gerald Ford, wife of the vice-president. Many organizations and groups have had parties here, and I've enjoyed meeting many people. From a personal standpoint, I haven't had a chance to do much entertaining, outside the official affairs, because I have such a busy schedule making speeches here and there. Then, too, I try to be here when the mansion is open to visitors three times a week. We have prison help, and the cook whom I trained was paroled, so she has gone.

"But as I said before, while we have been here the family has been closer together, and the children have been in and out. Amy, our little daughter, is with us here. One son, Chip, who has just gotten his masters' degree at Georgia State, and his wife, the former Caron Griffin of Hawkinsville, are going to Plains where Chip will work and Caron will be a first-grade teacher. Another son, Jack, is at law school in Athens where he and his wife, the former Judy Langford of Calhoun, live. Our son Jeffrey, who is working in

Plains this summer, will be going to the University of Georgia in the fall.

And now for the big question, "Would Rosalynn Carter like to be First Lady again?"

She said, "Let me put it this way: I wish every woman could have the wonderful experience of being the First Lady of Georgia one time in her life, and I think one term is just right." [1]

---

[1] After Jimmy Carter's term as governor of Georgia, he told his mother that he was going to run again. "For what?" she asked. "For president of the United States." The rest is history. The Carters lived in The White House from 1977-1981.

Now, he is still a spoke in the national political machine. The Carters live in their home in Plains, Georgia.

Prince Charming Visits

October 25, 1977

ENGLAND'S PRINCE CHARMING has left town, but the memories of young Charles linger on.

Here are some tidbits from the party at the Governor's Mansion and from the party at the Historical Society and the Swan House.

Atlanta's Margaret Perrin, whose piano talents have brightened parties for VIPs just about everywhere, was playing some popular, snappy tunes during the dinner at the mansion. She said later, "I was playing popular tunes, as I do all the time, when the Prince (of Wales and Earl of Chester—the titles *must* go together, according to British protocol) looked at me and winked and rubbed his brow, as if he were indicating he was very warm. In a few minutes, one of the waiters came over to the piano and served me a glass of champagne, and said, 'With the compliments of His Royal Highness.' That gave me a chuckle, thinking that the waiter was being nice saying that.

"Later, however, I was told that His Royal Highness really did suggest that I be served some champagne, as he suspected that all that playing made me overly warm."

Later, as he mingled with the guests throughout the

Yolande exchanges stories with Prince Charles

mansion, it was just like an Atlanta cocktail party—with the exception of one item of attire. His Royal Highness was wearing what we Americans call dancing pumps. His, however, were made of needlepoint, with the design on the toes done in the two plumes indicating his royal station.

Governor and Mrs. Busbee arranged for Mr. and Mrs. Allan Gray to have as their house guest on Valley Road Stephen Barry, valet to the prince. Mr. Gray, a Scotsman, had on his formal, plaid jacket.

Saturday at the Swan House, Philip Shutze was as proud as a peacock when His Royal Highness arrived at the elegant mansion. Mr. Shutze designed it for the late Mr. and Mrs. Edward Inman in the late twenties.

Before arriving at the Swan House itself, the prince walked

among masses of people in the west gardens of the home, speaking and shaking hands with some. One woman in the crowd was Britisher Mrs. Cecilia Summers who, as a member of the Daughters of the British Empire, was among those accorded tickets of admission to this gathering.

"His Royal Highness turned and spoke to me after I snapped his picture. He reached over and touched the golden pin I was wearing and asked me what it meant. I told him my late husband, Melton Summers, was presented with the pin of the Excellent Corps by the Chinese Imperial Government."

Yolande's Atlanta

Social Landmarks

West Peachtree? Here's How It Was Named

June 26, 1977

L AWD, MISS SCARLETT, they is tearing up Peachtree again!"

"True, so true, Mammy."

And so, a newcomer would say, "Peachtree? *West* Peachtree? How come?"

So here's a brief little history lesson for today:

Way back, Peachtree Road (now West Peachtree) ran a straight course, but it dipped into a deep "bottom" beyond the present junction with Peachtree Street. The road was a short, but well-traveled, route used by farmers and others bringing their produce into town as well as carrying their supplies back home.

When the rains came, that deep bottom became such a hazard that a team of horses couldn't have pulled through. So what did those sturdy early Atlantans do? They took the high road toward the east. Naturally, that was called Peachtree also, when drivers followed the ridge until the low ground of the original Peachtree was passed and their alternate route rejoined the original one. When both Peachtrees became bona fide byways, need arose for a different name for one of them. The original Peachtree was the one renamed, and, since it was on the west side of the city, it became known as West Peachtree.

Letter Throws New Light on Wren's Nest

November 2, 1975

OLD-HOME NOSTALGIA is making news this week. Although the birthday of Joel Chandler Harris is not until December 9, his home in West End, called the "Wren's Nest", has prompted the following never-before-published excerpt of a letter written over a quarter of a century ago.

Turning back the pages of history to update the story, Joel Chandler Harris, creator of the Uncle Remus stories, was born December 9, 1845, somewhere near Eatonton in Putnam County. After working on numerous newspapers in the South, Harris and his wife, the former Esther La Rose, moved to Atlanta in 1876.

Now for the nostalgia. A letter from Mrs. J. A. Redfearn in Albany brings an interesting sidelight. It is a letter written by her oldest aunt to her youngest aunt and is dated 1942. It says, in part, "Dear Jessie, I don't know how many Muses went to Atlanta from Lafayette, Alabama . . . they were closely identified with the early struggles of homemaking in a strange town which Sherman had recently devastated . . . Uncle Van Epps was fortunate in having two houses that escaped destruction . . . in town and another, a small frame cottage in the suburbs, in the section known as Sherman-

'Wren's Nest,' Joel Chandler Harris' home in West End

town. He let Father have the use of this house. . . .

"I do not know how long we lived in this house in Shermantown, but certainly for some months. . . . Father bought a five-acre plot of land in West End, built a small frame house and we settled there.

"The beginning of the house was very modest, only two large rooms placed end to end and a long room quite separate from the main building and used as a kitchen and dining room."

The "Jessie" to whom the letter was written was Miss Jessie Muse, for many years the principal of old Girls' High School, an important part of the city's early educational history. (George Muse, who founded the present George Muse Clothing Co., was also a member of this family.) The writer of the letter was Anna Muse, who later married Dr. O. E. Brown of Vanderbilt University. The house in the letter is the "Wren's Nest," the Harris home on Gordon Street in what is now West End.

Pappenheimer Home Was Musical Center

May 6, 1973

A LONG ABOUT the turn of the century, Mr. and Mrs. Oscar Pappenheimer built their colonial-style home "way out" on Ponce de Leon Avenue.

Soon afterward, it was ravaged by fire. But the Pappenheimers, undaunted, had it rebuilt and lived in it for many happy years. Their two children were born there, as were their two grandchildren.

The house is still standing, erect and beautiful, with the shade of beautiful trees, but the neighborhood has changed. The neighboring homes are gone, with one exception. The Edward Peters home at the corner of Ponce de Leon and Piedmont avenues is still there and, though empty, is still a Victorian monument to the past.[1]

The Pappenheimer home is now the Ponce de Leon Infirmary.[2]

In addition to social gatherings, the Pappenheimer home was the center for many cultural and musical events. For over thirty years, the owners opened their home every Monday

---

[1] It is now The Mansion Restaurant.
[2] It is now called the Mid-Town Hospital.

Music resounded through the Pappenheimer home on Ponce de Leon

evening for concerts, which the press of the day considered brilliant and unsurpassed in the city's history. Since leading figures in the world of the arts were entertained there, the fame of these affairs was nationwide.

These Monday night concerts in the home were somewhat like private operas. Mr. Pappenheimer, one of the early members of the Piedmont Driving Club, was also a pioneer guarantor of the Metropolitan Opera during its first eight years here.

The music room of the home was always packed with social, cultural and musical leaders. In it were two specially built Steinway pianos, and over a large stained-glass window was a built-in pipe organ. The mahogany-paneled walls were, in actuality, cabinets with sliding doors, which contained Mr. Pappenheimer's large collection of the classics and modern compositions.

In addition, the owners had two cellos (Mr. Pappenheimer played one sometimes), two bass violins and four violins. Music lovers and members of society were lured there for social events, which ranged from birthday parties to formal, seated dinners.

The big entrance hall was flanked by a drawing room and a dining room, the latter featuring a large fireplace. In addition to the music room were the breakfast room, butler's pantry, and latticed-in back porch. In the basement were the servants' quarters and a large area which contained the motor which ran the pipe organ.

A large hall in the upstairs of the home led to four bedrooms, dressing rooms, baths, a nursery, a sleeping porch, and a screened-in porch. A "wine attic" held a great supply of imported and vintage wines; a skylight topped the room. An intercom system connected all the rooms.

Both Pappenheimer children, Marie and Jack, were born in this home. Marie became Mrs. Joseph Taylor. Jack married Catherine Perry; they lived in the home and their two daughters, Ann and Mimi, were born there. Jack and Catherine moved from the home in 1933 to a new house on Woodward Way which is now the home and studio of artist Comer Jennings.

"I can remember we had birthday parties at the Ponce de Leon home," said Mrs. Platter, formerly Mimi Pappenheimer and the only surviving member of the immediate Pappenheimer family. "Graham Jackson always came and played for us. One time Hoolie [the nickname for her grandmother, Mrs. Oscar Pappenheimer] was given a surprise party on her fiftieth birthday. Graham came to that one, too. Mother let me pass some of the hors d'oeuvres, then Ann and I sat on the stairway and watched the party goings-on and played a game trying to remember everybody's name. Hoolie loved to play mah-jongg and bridge, and she gave weekly parties. There were dinner parties almost every week, too. I'll never forget how our cook, Blanche Mason, made ice cream on the back porch and always let Ann and me lick the dasher."

At the time of Mr. Pappenheimer's death in 1917, he was a member of the Board of Education, of which he had served as a vice-president. He was also still a guarantor of the Metropolitan Opera Company. Mrs. Pappenheimer gave all of her husband's musical instruments and collections to the University of Georgia Music Department, which at the time was headed by Hugh Hodgson. Mr. Hodgson gave a concert in her honor in Athens the following year.

One item, however, did not go to the University. One of the Steinway pianos was given to the beloved grandchild, Mimi, now Mrs. Vann Platter, who has it along with one of the music stands in her town house. She also has a complete set of Limoges china from her grandparents' estate and a silver compote bearing the date 1850-1875.

Some of the other items in the home are still family-owned. Mrs. Pappenheimer's valued collection of ivory figurines was given to her grandson, Dr. Walter James III, who lives in San Diego, California. The great four-poster bed which was in the master bedroom is now owned by a great-granddaughter, Mrs. Scott Offen, the former Ann James. Vicki James, another great-granddaughter, and now Mrs. John B. Gillespie, has the parliament clock which hung on the stairway landing of the home and which bears the date 1830. Mr. and Mrs. Platter's daughter Katie, now Mrs. Chris McCluney, also a great-granddaughter, who lives in Franklin, New Hampshire, has the entire set of silver flatware belonging to her great-grandparents.

After Mr. Pappenheimer's death, Mrs. Pappenheimer lived in the home for several years and then went to live with her daughter, Marie Taylor, and her husband in their apartment at Peachtree and Sixteenth streets. She died in 1949.

"After Hoolie died, I think the organ was sold, as well as one of the pianos," said Mrs. Platter. "The house was occupied for several years by the KA fraternity at Tech. After that, it started life all over again, as a hospital."

During the years, additional columns had been added by the architectural firm of Hentz, Reid, Adler and Philip Shutze, Associate.

So, now, Mrs. Murdock Equen[3] picks up the story.

"Murdock [the late Dr. Equen] bought the place in 1936 and established the Ponce de Leon Eye, Ear, Nose and Throat Hospital. The house had to be gutted and completely renovated inside to fill hospital needs. Rooms and wings were added for hospital use, and the mahogany floors had to be ripped out. We gave the mahogany to Judge Sam Sibley, whose hobby was making furniture.

"We installed the Waterford crystal doorknobs in our home on Habersham Road. Two of the crystal chandeliers in the music room were sent to my brother-in-law, the late Standard Equen, to use in the Equen plantation home in Minter, Mississippi. My sister-in-law, Mrs. Equen Rhodes, still lives there.

"The two large lead urns which were on the steps at the front entrance were given to our daughter, Mrs. Perry Ballard, Jr., (the former Ann Equen), who has them at her home on Howell Mill Road."

When Dr. Equen died in 1964, Mrs. Equen sold the hospital to a group of doctors who had worked with him when he established the hospital, but the building still stands to recall memories of its musical past.

---

[3]Mrs. Murdock Equen died August 3, 1977.

Castles Inspired Rhodes Residence

June 24, 1973

O NCE UPON A TIME, an Atlanta couple made a trip along the Rhine River in Germany. Along the route they saw, and admired, medieval castles set off by terraced vineyards or steep crags.

Returning to Atlanta, they asked an architect to design them a castlelike house "way out in the country" on Peachtree. They were Mr. and Mrs. A. G. Rhodes, and today their castle still stands in its majestic glory on Peachtree amid a bustling business area called Rhodes Center.

"I think that the home they built is a composite of several castles they saw along the Rhine," said Eugene L. Pearce, Jr., only living grandchild of Mr. and Mrs. Rhodes. "I remember my grandfather said that when they were building the house, all their friends thought he was crazy to go so far out in the country."

The home, made of Stone Mountain granite, was built between 1901 and 1904, at a cost of around $150,000, according to family hearsay. It is six stories high, and when built it was on a hundred-acre tract. Part of that land is now Rhodes Center and Spring Street, and the Atlantic Steel Company stood on fifty acres of the original tract.

Rhodes home was inspired by castles along the Rhine River

On the first floor there were an entrance hall, living room, parlor, dining room, kitchen, pantry, breakfast room, the "gold room," and an informal den. This den was called the Indian Room, for the wallpaper was splashed with Indians, both on foot and on horseback.

There were five bedrooms and baths on the second floor and a billiard room and den on the third floor; the remaining floors became smaller as they neared the turrets.

As a little boy, Pearce remembers he and the family climbed the stairs to one of the roof levels to watch the disastrous fire of 1917, which leveled hundreds of homes in the Boulevard area.

There were many family gatherings on Sunday afternoons and birthdays were always celebrated with parties.

Pearce said he had a big party on his fourth birthday, and the fun was at its height when a thunderstorm broke and lightning hit one of the chimneys. Dust, soot and chips of granite filled the room. However, the small-fry were not cheated out of their birthday cake and ice cream, for the party was just moved to another level and another room.

He and his parents, Mr. and Mrs. Eugene Pearce, lived at the home. Later, his mother married John A. Perdue, Jr.; their daughter, Marion Wilmontine Perdue, was married at the home to Dr. William Duncan Owens of Savannah. Their wedding on April 9, 1924, was hailed as one of the outstanding social events of the season. Dr. Owens was the son of Mrs. W. W. Owens and the late Mr. Owens.

The write-up, which appeared on the society pages of the *Atlanta Journal* of that date, said in part, "The entire lower floor of the home was lavish with green palms, foliage plants, southern smilax and gorgeous spring blossoms. The ceremony was in the entrance hall and the altar was before the mantel, which held palms, smilax and massive cathedral candelabra with white tapers. Showers of Easter lilies fell from brackets at either side of the altar.

"Leide's Orchestra [the late Enrico Leide] was in the rear hall, screened by tall palms. Members of the bridal party descended the wide, winding mahogany stairway. The bride was with her uncle, Joseph D. Rhodes, who gave her in marriage. The best man was Henry Dunn of Savannah."

It is interesting, from today's viewpoint, to read the description of the bride's bouquet. It stated, "Her bouquet was a cascade of orchids, white roses, and valley lilies, showered with spray orchids and valley lilies reaching to the floor."

The ribbon bearers were Katherine Flagler (now Mrs. William McClain) and Mary Meador Goldsmith (Mrs. James Campbell), and the junior bridesmaid was Josephine

Crawford (Mrs. James D. Robinson, Jr.). The flower girls were Tommie Perdue Quinn (Mrs. Fred Eve) and Isabel Boykin (Mrs. Robert Hamilton), and Beverly Rogers (Mrs. Francis Carter Wood of New Canaan, Connecticut) was train bearer.

The former Miss Perdue was president of the Atlanta Debutante Club of 1921-1922 and made her bow at a ball at the Piedmont Driving Club. She went to Washington Seminary and later was a member of the Junior League.

Rhodes, whose genius for business led him to amass a fortune in furniture and real estate, grew up in Henderson, Kentucky, a small town on the Ohio River. According to his grandson, Pearce, he remembered his boyhood impressions of the war years in that border state, where he often saw both Union and Confederate soldiers. He was definitely a Southerner. He moved to Atlanta in 1873 and opened his first store two years later. In his mind was always the thought that he wanted his own memorial to the Confederacy.

That memorial turned out to be one of the most fantastic, unusual and imaginative in the annals of history: he installed stained-glass windows in his home to portray the rise and fall of the Confederacy.

Forty years after the fall of the Confederacy, Mr. Rhodes engaged a first-rate artisan from Tiffany's in New York to design and execute three stained-glass windows. He spent forty thousand dollars on the picture, creating in his home the world's costliest private memorial to the Confederacy.

The first picture, at the bottom of the winding, handcarved mahogany stairway, shows the inauguration of Jefferson Davis as president of the Confederacy. The center panel shows General Stonewall Jackson during the height of the First Battle of Manassas. The third picture, at the top of the stairs, depicts General Robert E. Lee's farewell to his troops. The picture was skillfully placed so that the afternoon sun illuminated the figure of General Lee and softened the subdued figures of his men. Seals of the Confederacy are on each panel, along with the likenesses of several Confederate leaders. Legend has it that Mr. Rhodes sent back the sketches of the First Manassas several times to the Tiffany artists to be redone. The Yankees were not running fast enough!

After Mr. Rhodes' death in 1928, his heirs turned the mansion over to the state Department of History and Archives. It is still owned by the state, but now the stairway and the stained-glass windows have been installed in the new Archives Building. As Rhodes would have liked, the windows are destined to speak for the Lost Cause for years to come. They also stand as a memorial to an outstanding man—A. G. Rhodes.

Only Memories Occupy
the Former
Fitzhugh Knox Home

August 5, 1973

BACK IN OCTOBER of 1888, a young man named
Fitzhugh Knox boarded the train in his native
Richmond, Virginia, and headed toward Atlanta. In his
reminiscences, written and given to the Atlanta Historical
Society, he said he took the longest possible route to Atlanta
mainly to see the countryside. The route took him to
Lynchburg, to Cleveland, Tennessee, to Dalton and then
here.

He carved, through building, a permanent and notable
niche in the foundations of his adopted city. At the time of
his death in 1940, he was hailed as having been in the real
estate and building business longer than any other individual
in Atlanta at that time. Many apartment buildings still stand
as monuments to his business acumen.

He began building houses prior to 1892. His first
building was on the site of the old capitol, on the southwest
corner of Marietta and Forsyth streets. He built for the
property owners a two-story building, with six stores on the
first floor and offices upstairs. It was known as the Peoples
Building. When inquiring about renting the offices, people
would say, "What? Way up *there?*"

The last apartment he built was at 2650 Peachtree Road. In his long career of building homes and apartments, he made front-page news with one at the corner of Peachtree and Fifteenth streets: it was the "farthest out" building on the north side of town.

In 1891 Lena Reynolds Barber and Fitzhugh Knox were married at St. Phillips Episcopal Church, which was at the intersection of Hunter and Washington streets. It later became the Cathedral of St. Philip, now located on Peachtree Road at Andrews Drive in Buckhead. Mr. and Mrs. Knox built a home on Euclid Avenue in Inman Park where "just about everybody" lived. As the years passed, the city was spreading northward. So were many homeowners, including Mr. and Mrs. Knox.

Mr. Knox built his fine home way out on Piedmont Avenue. It was near Tenth Street and the carline just went to Fourteenth Street. The family moved into the new home in 1909. This is the story of that home when it was lived in and enjoyed by Mr. and Mrs. Knox and their nine children.

The children include the late Mrs. Thomas Lee Barber (Jennie Knox), the late Inman Knox, the late Fitzhugh Knox, Jr., the late John Somerville Knox, Olmsted Knox of Silver Spring, Maryland, Britton Knox, Mrs. Cecil Powell (Evelyn Knox) of Jacksonville, Florida, Mrs. G. Ray Mitchell (Helena Knox) and Mrs. Charles Luckie (Suzanne Knox) of Jacksonville.

Only memories occupy the home now, for after the death of Mr. Knox, the house was sold to the Family Services and now stands vacant.

The handsome, white home on the east side of the street is on an elevated lot. It is a frame house with four Corinthian columns across the front, and seven along the side porch and the porte-cochère.

The huge entrance hall on the first floor is somewhat like a rotunda, half surrounded by Corinthian columns. Also, on the first floor are a bedroom, den, two baths, parlor, dining room, living room, butler's pantry, kitchen, and a back porch. On the second floor are seven bedrooms, three baths, and a small balcony over the front door. Three more bedrooms and a bath are on a third floor. In the basement are a laundry room and bath. Two servants' rooms are over the two-car garage. There was a hole in the back yard for storing gasoline.

To say that there was constant activity in the home is quite an understatement. Nine children meant nine birthday parties each year, and those were added to all the other things going on.

Christmas was always an exciting time, with Mr. Knox

heading the family procession down the stairs into the living room where there was a big tree. One of the few rules from Mr. Knox was that the children and their friends must not run down the bank or park in the driveway.

During World War I a group calling themselves the Sammy Sisters (Uncle Sam's helpers) met at the Knox home to snip cloth into strips to make pillows, and to roll paper to use as tapers instead of matches. Then there were oyster suppers and bazaars to raise money for the Women of St. Luke's Church to give toward the Good Shepherd mural by Edwin Blashfield, which still hangs over the altar at the church. It was given in memory of the Reverend Robert Barrett, who filled the pulpit and the hearts of St. Luke's for many years. Mr. and Mrs. Knox had transferred their membership to St. Luke's from the church where they were married because St. Luke's was within walking distance.

The Knox home was the scene of many social affairs during the years. Mrs. Knox gave many mother-daughter teas as well as parties for the brides-to-be of the times. One daughter, Lena, had a playhouse in the back yard which was about the size of a one-car garage, filled most of the time by her playmates. Another daughter, Jennie, was a member of the first Atlanta Debutante Club. She made her debut at a reception in the home, and later was married there. When Evelyn Knox married Cecil Powell, that ceremony was also at the home. Another daughter, Suzanne, lived there during her debut year but made her bow at the Piedmont Driving Club.

Daughter Lena and her friend and neighbor Frances Howard made their debut together at a large reception at the Knox home, given by their mothers, Mrs. Knox and Mrs. C. B. Howard. In the social custom of the times, they received hundreds of guests while standing before masses of greens and flowers sent to the two debutantes. Frances Howard is now Mrs. Dupuis McLamb of Savannah.

There were parties given by the Pirate Club, a popular group of high-school belles, and by the sorority which three of the daughters, Lena, Evelyn and Suzanne, had joined at the Washington Seminary. Also in the custom of the era, Sunday afternoons saw the Knox home filled with fraternity friends who went calling from home to home.

Mr. Knox, who was also an expert in classical literature, was a historian as well as a member of the Society of Cincinnati, an organization of descendants of officers who fought in the American Army during the Revolution. The big home still stands as a great memorial to its builder.

King Home Is Still Regal Residence

June 17, 1973

SOON AFTER THE TURN of the century, a young couple of the city started planning a home which they dreamed of as a haven of happiness. The dream came true.

Mr. and Mrs. Clyde L. King had a large lot at the corner of Ponce de Leon Avenue and Oakdale Road. Together, they planned their big Georgian home with its six perfect Corinthian columns. Built of old Georgia red bricks, the house had thirteen rooms in all and expansive gardens and lawns.

Today the home is known throughout the United States by every woman who is a member or an alumna of the ADPi sorority.

In 1910 it was completed, and Mr. and Mrs. King moved in, the first family to occupy a home in the section which was being developed as Druid Hills. The street number then was 1010 Ponce de Leon Avenue, a number better known to some Atlantans than 1600 Pennsylvania Avenue in Washington, D. C. Furnished in elegant taste, the home was filled with many family pieces plus many antiques Mrs. King bought in New Orleans.

1010 Ponce de Leon was for years a gathering place for

King home is now national headquarters for ADPi sorority

many groups of Atlanta society. Since Mr. King was owner of the King Plow Company, the house also became a setting for events given for visiting officials and friends.

Sunday and Friday night gatherings saw many students from Emory University as well as friends of the Kings enjoying their hospitality, while picnics, garden parties and afternoon teas were part of Atlanta's social history. And those were the days, too, when afternoon bridge parties were among favorite types of entertainment. Mrs. King planned Christmas dinners for as many as forty-five guests with as much ease as she planned for Mr. King and their two daughters and two sons.

One of the daughters, Irene King, married George Woodruff in a sparkling wedding in the home, coming down the massive stairway into the drawing room for the ceremony. Afterwards there was a reception.

The second daughter of the family, Clara Belle King, made her debut in the home as a member of the Atlanta Debutante Club. Later she became the bride of the late Dr. William Troy Bivings, Jr., at a wedding at the home. She, too, came down the big stairway into the drawing room to make her vows in a beautiful ceremony.

The elder son of the family, the late Clyde L. King, Jr., and his fiancée, Frances Poole, had their wedding rehearsal party at the King home, one of the larger social affairs given there. They married the next day at the Poole home, Ovidia, at one of the brilliant weddings of 1924. Frances King (now Mrs. Ed Garlington) was the women's trapshooting champion of the world and is in the Trapshooting Hall of Fame.

The younger son, the late John King, made the headlines one year in the twenties when he rode his pony in a big carnival given by the Agnes Scott alumnae and held in the park across the street from the King home.

Mrs. King's garden was one of the showplaces of the city, and featured three connecting pools. In the early 1920s the city of Atlanta and the Georgia Power Company began their annual prize contest for the best outdoor lighted Christmas tree. Mrs. King was the first winner, receiving a prize of twenty-five dollars, and continued to win for many years.

Mrs. King, the former Clara Belle Rushton, died in 1939, and the following spring, when the garden was in full bloom, King opened it to the public in his wife's memory. A replica of the entrance to the home was designed as the King monument in Oakland Cemetery. This was King's wish; since they couldn't bring her home, they would take a touch of home to her. He died in 1941.

The home remained in the King family until 1943.

In March 1955, the big house again became a status symbol of Atlanta. It was dedicated as the national headquarters of the oldest secret society for college women in the United States—the Alpha Delta Pi sorority.

The sorority was founded at Wesleyan College in Macon in 1851, and its long and colorful life reached a peak when the King home became its memorial headquarters. Thus the house began Phase Two of its long and distinguished life.

The home still stands in its original majestic glory. An entire wing is occupied by the executive offices of the sorority. Upstairs bedrooms are for visiting VIPs. On the main floor the formal rooms are still elegantly furnished. Many of the original items of the King era have been retained, such as a hand-carved gold-leaf Italian mirror, several crystal chandeliers, a Sheraton buffet, and Chippendale chairs and table in the dining room, as well as a Chinese Chippendale mirror, an Empire-style chaise sofa and gold leaf wall sconces in the Prince of Wales plume pattern. In addition, there are silver tea and coffee services, pitchers, goblets, trays, an antique brass inkwell, a silver serving basket, French porcelain urns, a Coalport compote, and other accessories and furnitue which have been given by ADPi alumnae as personal and memorial gifts.

Mrs. King's garden is now known as the Hubbard Memorial Garden, in memory of Minnie Allen Hubbard, of Montclair, New Jersey, a past president of ADPi.

And one more change: the house everyone knew as the King home, at 1010 Ponce de Leon Avenue, is now one of three national sorority headquarters, and has become 1386 Ponce de Leon Avenue.

Craigellachie,
John W. Grant Home,
Is Now Private Club

May 20, 1973

THERE IS THE STORY about the man who was taking an out-of-town client to lunch.

He drove out West Paces Ferry Road to the intersection of Andrews Drive and turned right through big stone columns into a wide, winding driveway.

"Do you have friends who live *here?*" gasped the visitor. "This is a mansion!"

Yes, it was a mansion, but it is now the Cherokee Town Club, with some fifteen hundred members, and is an elegant place for these members to lunch.

There are many Atlantans who can remember when they did have friends living in the mansion, before it became a swank social and private club.

It was Craigellachie, the English-country-style home of Mr. and Mrs. John W. Grant. The name was taken from the mountain in Scotland that had been for generations the meeting place of the clan of Grant.

The white stucco and limestone house was erected between 1914 and 1917. The grounds—some one hundred acres—had the proportions of a vast country estate. The gardens looked like pictures in seed catalogues; they were so

Craigellachie, former home of Mr. and Mrs. John W. Grant

immaculate and so perfect in seasonal coloring and beauty. Mrs. Grant was a member of the Peachtree Garden Club, and she opened her gardens during the first Georgia Garden Pilgrimage in 1937, sponsored by the Garden Clubs of Georgia.

In addition to the gardens, formal and cutting, there was a large lily pond and tennis courts on the property.

Craigellachie was the scene of many social events during the years. Mr. and Mrs. Grant entertained a great deal; their luncheons during Atlanta's opera seasons of years past were gala events. One of the brilliant social affairs they gave was the reception to celebrate their silver wedding anniversary. Guests wore their wedding attires of bygone days.

The elder daughter of the family, Margaret, married

Richard Wilmer at the home, with a reception following the ceremony. The younger daughter, Anne, was married to Frank C. Owens at the First Presbyterian Church and their wedding reception was held at the home.

The home had a ballroom on the first floor, along with a parlor, den, living room, entrance hall with twin stairways, pantry, dining room, kitchen, and breakfast room. Upstairs there were five large bedrooms and baths, two small bedrooms, a nursery and a billiard room, plus a large upstairs hall.

Mr. and Mrs. Owens and their family lived at the home until 1954 when they moved to a house on Blackland Road. The late John Grant, Jr., lived there until 1956.

Mr. Grant, builder of Craigellachie, was a leading Atlanta businessman; among his many affiliations, he was a trustee of Georgia Tech. In this capacity he gave fifty thousand dollars to the college toward the cost and development of the athletic field, named Grant Field as a memorial to his son, Hugh Inman Grant.

So, now, what about the Cherokee Club?

Back in 1955 some two hundred people gathered in the Ida Williams Library in Buckhead to form a new social club for the city. One of them was Mrs. James E. Williams, who was credited with founding the enterprise. She made her first speech that rainy afternoon outlining the plans for the club.

The meeting was such a success that before it ended many had donated to the organization fund and signed membership applications. The club was to become a reality. And the site? Almost in the center of Buckhead for the town club, and a big, sprawling site in Sandy Springs for the country club in the near future. Negotiations got under way with John W. Grant, Jr., for an arrangement to lease, with option to buy, his family estate.

The Cherokee Club adopted its charter in 1956 with six

hundred and twenty-three approved members. Howard L. Stillwell, Jr., was named the first president, and Mrs. Williams, who had chartered the club's formation, was made the first honorary member of the board. The yext year the club began building its eighteen-hole golf course at the country-club site in Sandy Springs.

The Grant home was bought for the town club, and had its face lifted to comply with club activities. However, it still retains its beauty and elegance. When built, the house had some twenty thousand feet of floor space.

Remaining in their original state with some of the original furnishings are the entrance hall, where the magnificent twin stairway is located, and the library. Walls in the entrance hall are dark mahogany. The stone mantel is made with the same type of cream-colored limestone used to build Westminster Abbey, Canterbury Cathedral, and others among England's greatest churches.

Adjoining this room is the former ballroom of the Grants, which is now the cocktail lounge. The club has added a tremendous wing to the original home which is now the main dining room, with a seating capacity of five hundred. This connects with the club's new ballroom, also an addition. Former upstairs bedrooms are now private dining rooms, a ladies' lounge, a men's sitting room, a game room, and a pool room. The north wing is strictly for men, serving as their private domain for card playing, pool, etc.; there is also a bar.

Swimming pools are at the rear of the property, and tennis courts at the side. Re-landscaped grounds provide parking areas. Social affairs occur around the clock at Cherokee. The club is noted for its annual Wassail Ball, a traditional Old English extravaganza held at Christmas time. This has become so popular that for the past several years it has been held on two consecutive evenings. There are seasonal balls and parties and the usual brunches during football season.

The Cherokee Club occupies a very special place in Atlanta's social history. In April of 1964, Mrs. E. T. Barwick, Mrs. R. K. Hancock, and Mrs. Granville Tabb, Jr., were appointed by the board to formulate plans for a debutante group composed of daughters of members. Mrs. Chess Lagomarsino and Mrs. Philip White became social advisors of the debutante activities.

So, on June 10, 1964, the Cherokee Debutantes were formally presented to the entire membership at a reception and a ball. It marked the first time in Atlanta's social history that a private club had its own debutante club within its membership.

The girls were wined and dined through the years as they made social history. But in May of 1972, it was announced that the Cherokee Town and Country Club had dropped its 1972 debutante program due to a "disappointing response by eligible daughters [of members] to make a debut." At the time, club president Thomas A. Slaughter, Jr., said that it was not a permanent measure, and that the Cherokee Debutantes would appear on the social stage again someday.

Pinebloom, Home of the Preston Arkwrights

May 13, 1973

FOR NEARLY half a century, the big English-style mansion on Ponce de Leon Avenue in the Druid Hills section was the setting for some of the city's top social events and the launching pad for many organizations.

Its name was Pinebloom, and it was the home of Mr. and Mrs. Preston S. Arkwright, the former serving at one time as the president of the Georgia Power Company.

The home is still standing, like a mighty social fortress, but some changes have been made, including an addition. The addition is the Jackson Hill Baptist Church.

The story begins long before the late Preston Arkwright built his big English-style home. His grandfather, Richard Arkwright of Preston, England, had been knighted by Queen Victoria. His father, Richard Arkwright, moved to Savannah, Georgia, where he had vast acreage in a rice plantation; his ties with his native England were still strong, and he named his son Preston for his home town. Young Preston was orphaned at the age of seven and was sent to the Catholic orphanage in Sharon, Georgia. As an older boy he went to North Georgia College in Dahlonega.

Money was scarce for the young boy, and in order to go to

Pinebloom, whose name was inspired by golden pollen

the university he taught Latin, math, and dancing to work his way through college. His family says he often said he nearly starved to death, but starving or not, he managed to graduate and gave the baccalaureate sermon at his commencement.

He married Dorothy Colquitt, whose father, Alfred Colquitt, was a U. S. senator and a governor of Georgia.

Their big home, built in 1915, had six bedrooms, six baths and dressing rooms, two sleeping porches, an attic, a ballroom, entrance hall, drawing room, library, dining room, sunroom, breakfast room, kitchen and an assortment of closets. The entrance hall was done in imported oak paneling taken from a castle on the Rhine River. A frieze around the top was a canvas painting by a German artist, and in the living room was a mantel of pink Georgia marble. The library contained all the books which had belonged to Alfred Colquitt.

Mr. and Mrs. Arkwright's daughter, Dorothy, made her debut at Pinebloom at an elaborate afternoon reception in 1917, followed by a dance for the young set in the ballroom on the third floor. Two years later, in 1919, Dorothy married Captain Glenville Giddings, who was in the medical corps overseas during World War I, at an elaborate wedding in the spacious living room. The next day was Easter, so all the wedding flowers, Easter lilies, were given to the First Methodist Church.

The son of the family, the late Preston S. Arkwright, Jr., also married there in the early twenties. His bride was Ann Stringfellow, and their ceremony was followed by a reception. When the former Julia Dunning married Alfred Colquitt, who was a brother of Mrs. Arkwright, the wedding reception was held there. She is now Mrs. Prince Webster.

"I can't remember when there wasn't some party given at home," said Mrs. Giddings at her present home on Northside Drive. "In addition to the social events Mother and Father gave, there were Easter-egg hunts for the children at the Dorothy Arkwright Day Nursery, which was named for Mother. It later became a part of the Sheltering Arms. Mother was also in a group called the Order of Old-Fashioned Women, which spearheaded the formation of the Sheltering Arms. She gave many baby parties for grandchildren of the members. Nurses brought the babies and they played out on the lawn.

"There were no fraternity houses at Emory at that time, and frat men would gather at our home for meetings and for parties. Father was a Sigma Nu and my brother Preston was a Chi Phi. Men from those and other fraternities would come to the house during the weekend for supper." (Mrs. Pearl Hyde, who was housemother for the Chi Phis for over twelve years, always came along with her "boys," as she called them.)

After the death of Mr. and Mrs. Arkwright, Pinebloom was saved from a bulldozer's fate. It was sold in 1964 to the Jackson Hill Baptist Church. The revolving bookcase which was in the library and which Mrs. Giddings' grandfather, Alfred Colquitt, used while a senator in Washington and while a governor here, is now in Mrs. Giddings' home. So is the handsome Adam-style sideboard which had been in the dining room. A wrought-iron gazebo which was in the garden at Pinebloom is now in the garden beside the pool at the present home of Mrs. Giddings.

Reverend C. Michael Warr is the pastor of the Jackson Hill Baptist Church, which is a brick wing of Pinebloom.

"The old Arkwright home was first used as the Southern Baptist Radio Commission of the Southern Baptist Convention," said Reverend Warr. "It was Dr. Sam Lowe of the Inman Park Baptist Church who had the first Baptist Hour on radio. We have had the church here for sixteen years.

"The Sunday school is in the Arkwright home. So is the chapel where we have the Wednesday services, which is also available for small weddings and funerals. On the third floor there are some of the original studios of the commission.

"Our church was first on Boulevard, and many of our worshippers were student nurses and interns at Georgia Baptist Hospital. We still have some in our congregation, which stands now at four hundred and fifty. We consider ourselves one family in our church building where we moved in 1957."

Here is one more thing about the original mansion, Pinebloom. If you are wondering about the name, here is what Mrs. Giddings says: "It was named for the old Colquitt place in Albany. The legend says that when the pine pollen fell and was a deep gold, it signified richness in the nation. In other words, the pollen really 'bloomed.' The bloom, then, combined with the pine trees, resulted in its name, 'Pinebloom.' "

Trygveson, Home of the Andrew Calhouns, Is Known as Pink Palace

April 29, 1973

LANDMARKS, LIKE memories, are man's stake in the past.

And Atlanta has a rich heritage in them.

There are many social landmarks in the Atlanta area. They stand somewhat like citadels of society, as proud as their former owners. These stately homes are still occupied, but not by the families whose lives and activities are a part of the city's glamorous past.

The homes have a new outlook now. Some are churches, renovated in some parts, and some have new owners. One is a private club, one is a hospital, and one is the national headquarters of a sorority.

Atlanta is noted for her beautiful homes, and many of them have that unmatched and magical touch of Columbus-born Philip Shutze, one of the leading architects of this century.

In them have been many top social events of the past. During the heyday of entertaining at home, many weddings and debuts were at home, and many homes served as the birthplaces of groups and societies which were to chart the course of many of today's customs.

The Pink Palace is still a reigning queen

One of these homes is Trygveson, an Italian villa which blends into its Georgia setting to perfection. Atlanta's climate offers everything to simulate the colorings and characteristics of Italian country villas.

It was Shutze, also a genius with landscape architecture, who designed this Italian villa for Mr. and Mrs. Andrew Calhoun in 1922. Soon known as the Pink Palace, this house of plaster is tinted like the strata of Georgia clay, in tones mixed by Shutze himself to recapture the sun-parched Italian landscape. Viewed from West Paces Ferry Road, the entrance gates frame a dramatic view of the house and the sunken garden, set far back on a tree-shaded hill.

It was the place to see on those Sunday afternoons fifty years ago, and in later years, too, when the family took automobile rides "way out on West Paces Ferry Road." The Pink Palace was the target for all camera bugs and sightseers as well.

From the Villa Cuzzano near Verona, the Villa Gori at Siena, and the Villa Spade on the Janiculum came the inspiration for much of the architectural detail used in the house and the gardens. The baroque style of the house is continued in the architecture of the formal gardens and in the facade facing the road. Curving double stairs flanking a wall fountain descend from the high-walled terraces of the house to a garden of boxwood.

There is a semi-circular entrance court at the rear. On the downstairs floor are a ballroom, drawing room, dining room, entrance hall, breakfast room, powder room, pantry, kitchen, and screened porch. The second floor has five bedrooms, two sleeping porches, a sitting room and five baths. There is another bedroom and a laundry on the third floor.

It was in these rooms that Mr. and Mrs. Calhoun and their children, James, Abner, Louise, Catherine, and Nancy, enjoyed years of gracious living. As the children were growing up they played, and later had parties, in their "big" playhouse near the walled courtyard and enjoyed tennis on their private courts.

During the twenties when the Metropolitan Opera came to the city, the Calhouns had many lavish parties and in the custom of the era, the opera stars came and, as the saying goes, sang for their supper. The formality of the parties was lessened when stars like Enrico Caruso sang favorite arias.

It was also at this home that Atlanta's first garden club was formed. Mrs. Calhoun, the former Mary Guy Twiggs from Lookout Mountain, Tennessee, invited a group of her friends to come to Trygveson for high tea, for the purpose of forming a garden club "like we have at home." Thus, on a wintry March day in 1923, the Peachtree Garden Club was formed.

As the years passed, the young set, as well as friends of Mr. and Mrs. Calhoun, gathered for many happy times and parties at the big mansion. Two of the daughters married there, each descending a winding stairway to enter the drawing room where the ceremony took place. Catherine Calhoun married Dr. Fred Minnich in 1940, and two years later Nancy Calhoun married Charles Motz. The other daughter, Louise, chose New York for her marriage to Roby Robinson, Jr. When Mrs. Calhoun became a widow, Mr. and Mrs. Robinson moved into the home and lived there for several years carrying on the social tradition of the home. The Robinsons were victims of the jetliner crash at Orly Field in Paris in June 1962, which killed one hundred and six Atlantans returning from a European tour.

The two sons of the family, Abner and James Calhoun, live here. The former is married to Katherine Jetton. The former chatelaine of the home, Mrs. Calhoun, and her son, James, still live on West Paces Ferry Road, but in the home which was the residence of Mr. and Mrs. Robinson before they moved to the Pink Palace.

The Pink Palace is still a reigning queen, but time and progress have changed her domain. The vast frontage on West Paces Ferry Road and the winding driveway have a new look. Though Trygveson is still privately owned, the acreage has been subdivided. What was once the driveway is now Pinestream Road. The trees are still there along with many homes. Trygveson itself has a Pinestream Street number rather than one on West Paces Ferry Road.

The vista from West Paces Ferry Road, however, is still dramatic. Trygveson is still a beauty spot on the face of Atlanta.

The Swan House,
Showplace of Atlanta

THE SWAN HOUSE, one of the most elegant homes in
Atlanta as well as in the Southeast, is now owned and
preserved by the Atlanta Historical Society. More than one
hundred thousand visitors, from every section of the United
States and some ninety foreign countries, have toured the
magnificent building.

It faces Andrews Drive in northwest Atlanta. The facade of
the home is distinguished by a cascading series of basins with
water flowing from one to another. Retaining walls are
planted with colorful seasonal flowers and plants.

This Atlanta landmark, just past a half century in age, has
a fascinating background as a rare example of luxurious living
during an important era in the city's history.

Swan House was built in the 1920s as a residence for the
late Mr. and Mrs. Edward H. Inman and their family. Its
building cost was some five hundred thousand dollars, a mere
drop in the bucket compared to its current value. Completed
in 1928, it became the social center for many affairs hosted by
the Inmans. Mr. Inman was heir to an Atlanta fortune built
on cotton, banking, real estate, wholesale dry goods and

The Swan House is preserved by the Atlanta Historical Society

railroads. He lived to enjoy his home for only three years. Mrs. Inman lived there until she died in 1965.

When Mrs. Inman died, the Atlanta Historical Society bought the home and its eighteen surrounding acres, in its usual quest to save and preserve the architectural gems in the city's crown. The house is open to the public now, and visitors are awed with its beauty. James H. Grady, professor emeritus of Architecture at Georgia Tech, says it is "Atlanta's best design ensemble."

An Atlanta architect, Philip Trammell Shutze, designed the home. In 1915 he was awarded the Prix de Rome, the highest honor of the Ecole des Beaux Arts. He combined two styles when designing the Inman home, that of the famous Italian villas built by architect Andrea Palladio for Venetian noblemen, and that of eighteenth-century English country homes.

However, each room is clearly a twentieth-century creation of Mrs. Inman and her interior designers, and evokes the mood of a particular style. Eighteenth-century Palladianism is reflected in the spectacular entrance hall. Carved doorways surmounted by broken pediments flank a grand spiral stairway rising from a black and white marble floor. The library is done in the late seventeenth-century style. The beautiful proportions and details of the morning room introduce the clarity of an early eighteenth-century room.

Mrs. Inman enjoyed both the incorporation of the swan motif into the architectural detail and its continuation through furnishings collected in this country and in Europe. At least one swan can be found in each room.

In the dining room, the gaiety, fantasy and color of wallpaper painted in the Chinese style recall the glamorous attraction which the East held for Western eyes in the eighteenth century. The prizes of Mrs. Inman's collections are in this room—a pair of eighteenth-century console tables which are attributed to the London carver, Thomas Johnson. Each boasts extraordinary carvings of lifelike swans amidst reeds, rocks and water plants.

The following quotes from the book *Classical America IV* define the talent of Philip Shutze in the words of Henry Hope Reed:

To an age which has too often assumed that the classical period passed out of existence over a generation ago, it is always a surprise to learn that the tradition is still very much with us.

Nowhere is this more true in the western world than in the United States. Here, certain men have continued to design in the classical, thanks to a sympathetic patronage.

Such an architect is Philip Trammell Shutze. We are especially pleased to join with the Atlanta Historical Society in documenting and paying homage to the remarkable work of Philip Shutze.

His finest work in the first decade was unquestionably the Swan House, now owned by the Atlanta Historical Society.

Medical Academy, An Architectural Gem, Dedicated in 1941

January 17, 1974

OUT ON WEST PEACHTREE Street between Sixth and Seventh streets stands a big Greek Revival building which is the Academy of Medicine. It has been a part of Atlanta's life since its dedication a week after Pearl Harbor, on December 15, 1941.

A big reception featured the late Dr. Howard Hailey, president of the Fulton County Medical Society, as official host. A very special guest was Dr. Fred Rankin, president-elect of the American Medical Association, who came down from his home in Lexington, Kentucky, for the affair. After Dr. Louie Newton gave the devotional, guests wandered through the building to harp music by Winifred Shackelford (now Mrs. Waverly Brown). Dr. Allen Bunce, president of the Medical Association of Georgia, was greeting and shaking hands with all his medical cronies.

The Academy building was completed at an estimated cost of $150,000, including the lot. Greek Revival in style, it boasts a six-columned, pedimented portico offset by the Academy's insignia and reached by a flight of stone steps. This leads into a rotunda with a vaulted ceiling supporting a dome.

Academy of Medicine building has served many purposes

When it was built, the library was a memorial to Dr. Stewart Roberts. This space is now used for offices. Also marking the dedication was a chandelier, said to have come from an old home in Philadelphia, which was installed as a memorial to Dr. E. C. Davis. The chandelier was one hundred seventy-five years old and originated when gas first became employed as a source of light in 1796.

Now in the rotunda of the building is a handsome chandelier which was bought about thirty years ago, by friends of Dr. Davis, from the movie set of *Gone With the Wind*. According to some of the auxiliary's members, this chandelier hung at the foot of the long, winding stairway in the Atlanta mansion which Rhett Butler built for Scarlett. The chandelier was imported from Czechoslovakia.

The Academy of Medicine is the home of the Medical Association of Atlanta, which was organized in 1884 by twelve members who paid three dollars a month in dues. The members had trouble finding a meeting place which they could afford. In fact, up until 1889, they met at places like the old state capitol building at Marietta and Forsyth streets, the old YMCA building at Pryor and Auburn, the Knights of Pythias Hall in the old Connally Building at Whitehall and Alabama streets, a vacant room in the old Equitable Building, and a parlor in the Kimball House.

About that time Dr. E. C. Davis and Dr. L. C. Fisher (who formed the Davis-Fisher Sanitorium, which later became Crawford W. Long Hospital) came to the aid of the group. They offered the use of their offices in the Flatiron Building at Peachtree and Broad. In 1902, when the Carnegie Library (now the Atlanta Public Library) opened, the members were allowed to meet in the basement. It was not until 1923 that the group had its first permanent headquarters, a frame dwelling on Prescott Street which had been built by W. Woods White near the site of the present Crawford Long Hospital. In 1939 the Prescott building was sold to the hospital, and the present lot on West Peachtree Street was bought from the Peters Land Company

Ground was broken for the present building in June, 1941. Philip Shutze designed the building, with his firm of Hentz, Adler and Shutze as consultants: the architect was R. Kennon Perry. M. W. Wise was the heating contractor, but no air conditioning was planned at the time.

Since its dedication, the Academy has come a long way; there have been drives for funds and for various undertakings. The building has served many groups besides the medical society, which now numbers over twelve hundred members. It is the home base of the Atlanta Graduate Medical Assembly and the Community Health Planning Committee, and the meeting place for related groups, including the Northern District Dental Society and the Explorer Scouts.

Inside the building, students from area high schools can use a well-stocked library on medical history. This library was organized, decorated, furnished and made available to the schools in 1971 by Mrs. Milton B. Satcher, who was auxiliary president that year.

Mrs. George C. Callaway is auxiliary president this year. Dr. and Mrs. Ralph Murphy are co-chairmen for the Ball and are being assisted by Mrs. J. H. Wirth and Mrs. Glenn Bridges, Jr. Mrs. Joseph R. B. Hutchinson is in charge of the decorations, which will carry out a Dr. Zhivago theme of silver and white. Mrs. William Collins is program chairman.

Swan Coach House Is Now "The Place"

IT IS THE PLACE. The Place to have lunch. The Place to shop for universal gifts, even baby clothes. The Place to take friends, visitors and even your relatives.

It is The Place to be "glimpsed." If a bride doesn't have at least one pre-nuptial luncheon or shower there, there will be a cloud over her marriage for years to come. Some girls even marry in the garden there, with a reception afterwards. It becomes a marriage rite few others can claim.

The food at The Place is so marvelous that you automatically become a glutton, a sin you can brag about.

The Place, of course, is the Swan Coach House, opened October 1, 1967. And who makes it so magic? Women, that's who. Women whose feminine powers have established an up-to-date landmark unmatched in the city's annals. Funds running into the upper, upper thousands have been raised there, to be used for forwarding the visual arts at the Atlanta Memorial Arts Center.

The women who run the Coach House and raise money are the founding members of the Forward Arts Foundation, Inc. Their flea markets raise over fifty thousand dollars each fall.

Swan Coach House owes debt to the 'Darling Dozen'

So, who turned on the woman power? The women themselves.

Turn back the clock to the early 1950s. Things began to spark when the first Women's Committee of the High Museum of Art was formed by the late Mrs. Clifford Ragsdale. She suggested they have an auction on the front lawn of the museum, to lure Peachtree traffic—both walking and motorized. Mrs. Emory Cocke, one of the members, suggested a Flea Market, along with the auction. There was a lot of tall talk to a lot of people to do this, but the result speaks for itself—an approximate eighteen thousand dollars rolled in from the fleas and shoppers.

The home of the late Mr. and Mrs. E. P. McBurney, next to the temporary museum, was being used as a wing for the

[155]

display of paintings and objets d'art. Mrs. Emory Cocke and another committee member, Mrs. Isabelle Kennedy, had what you might call double vision (at the same time). They saw the McBurney carriage house at the rear of the property—wouldn't it be fun to use it for a tea room? Mrs. Sally (Granger) Hansell, as head of the museum's women's committee, knew what a success the auction and flea market had been and let the ladies have several thousand dollars to open their tea room. It was an instant success, somewhat like *Gone With the Wind*, when the tea room opened in October, 1957.

Some of the Women's Committee offered to be volunteer workers. An added attraction was Doris Cook, who had been highly recommended to Mrs. Cocke and Mrs. Kennedy as a "super chef." They finally lured her to join them at their pet project, which they named the "Coach House." Mrs. Cook's knack for turning just plain, good old food into scrumptious eating, soon turned the location into Atlanta's main noontime attraction. Every day was D-Day—Doris' delectable dishes.[1] It was very chic to work there, and museum visitors felt that lunch at the Coach House was a *must,* like paying the Internal Revenue.

One sunny day tragedy struck, in the form of progress. A bulldozer appeared, ready to crush everything in sight to make way for the long-awaited museum. Everything, including the Coach House, was doomed for crushing—all except the twelve women. "Do or die" was their attitude! The remedy? Another Coach House. To add insult to injury, Mrs. Cook had vanished, to take over a commercial job. After being warned of the advent of the bulldozer, the volunteers had grabbed everything they could carry, even the iron

---

[1]Mrs. Carolyn Clayton is now director of the restaurant.

hitching post Mrs. Clifford Ragsdale had donated for the entrance walkway.

Each of the twelve women became a mythical FBI agent in search of a new Coach House. They had their bank account of seven thousand dollars.

Because the twelve had decided to pull the plug of membership in the Women's Committee of the High Museum of Art, they were labeled the "Dirty Dozen." They couldn't have cared less (except that Doris Cook had left). The Dirty Dozen got a charter as the Forward Arts Foundation, Inc., on September 21, 1965, making it a date to remember.

Recognition of the Dirty Dozen is now due. They are Mrs. Ivan Allen, Jr.; Mrs. Philip Aston, Jr.; Mrs. James V. Carmichael; Mrs. Anne Cox Chambers; Mrs. Emory Cocke; Mrs. Richard Courts, Jr.; Mrs. Frank Ferst; Mrs. Woolford Kennedy; Mrs. Baxter Maddox; Mrs. O. Ray Moore; Mrs. Charles B. Nunnally; and Mrs. James D. Robinson.

Mrs. Anne Cox Chambers was the first chairman of the board of trustees of the Forward Arts Foundation, Inc. When Jimmy Carter became president of the United States, he appointed her ambassador to Belgium.

Another of the current members is Mrs. Julian Carr, but she has another claim to fame. As a member of the Cherokee Garden Club, she founded the first total garden library in the city. It is located in McElreath Hall of the Atlanta Historical Society. The library is staffed by Cherokee Garden Club members. So, if your petunias get sick or your magnolia trees bear red blossoms instead of white, rush to the garden library's medical section!

Meanwhile, as the women searched for another place to open and operate, fate was shuffling up a new deal to play. A charming little white house on West Paces Ferry Road, a block west from Peachtree Road, was a future target for the bulldozer. The house was at one time the home of Mr. and Mrs. Thomas Cassels and their daughter, Elizabeth, now Mrs. Richard Rubenoff. The Dirty Dozen grabbed it at once as a temporary place to open shop again. (The Cassels home was torn down to make way for the extension of Slaton Drive into West Paces Ferry Road.) To add to their delight, they became mythical FBI agents again and tracked down Doris Cook, to make the place the most important and best eating place in town.

The Dirty Dozen were closer to their goal than they realized. In the wooded area just to the north stood a garage and servants' quarters, on the Edward Inman property which had just been bought by the Atlanta Historical Society in 1966. To those never-say-die women, it was like finding oil spurting up in their front yard.

Another garage! Somebody was on their side.

They obtained it. Woman-power was turned on again. And almost before you could yell, "Hallelujah!" the place, down at the heels, was transformed into its present look. The exterior and interior were painted, remodeling and additions were completed, and the porch enclosed. That same hitching post from the first Coach House still guards the entrance. Members of the Iris Garden Club, who polished up the landscaping at the first house, have worked again on the front and sides.

The "new" Coach House was designed by the noted local architect Philip Shutze as he was drawing plans for the Inman home in the late 1920s.

The Dirty Dozen are very happy in their new place, which is within waving distance of the elegant Swan House. Mrs. Cocke is back, selecting all those fascinating gifts in the Coach House Shop adjoining the eating area. Along with Mrs. H. J. Crawford, she goes to New York twice a year as a clever, twentieth-century merchant who knows what

Atlantans and visitors will buy—and do they buy! A gift from the Coach House, with its little pink seal, is like something from the White House or the Queen.

The volunteer list for the shop includes the top names of the city, who, along with the Dirty Dozen and associate members, make a great team. Volunteers also help in the dining room, which is packed Monday through Saturday.

The dining room is so colorful and attractive, it looks as though the interior designer and the florist have just left. The downstairs pub has a paisley covering on its walls and opens onto a small terrace overlooking a sprawling half-moon garden with a carpet of grass.

The garden edging, designed by Mrs. Charles Parham, is a real beauty spot. Outlined with hosta, it is backed with small clusters of white petunias and small boxwood plants. Centering the half-moon circle are the handsome gates, which were formerly in the lobby of the De Give Opera House when it was built in 1893. The theater in downtown Atlanta has been torn down. The gates were given in 1971 by Pauline De Give Wellborn and Marshall Wellborn in memory of her parents, Henry and Katherine De Give.

Upstairs there is a private dining room for parties, a glass-enclosed front porch, and the "members's room" which opens onto a second-story terrace.

An art gallery has been added onto the east side of the building.

So ends the story of the Darling Dozen—as they should be called instead of "Dirty," such a dirty word for such chic, smart and prominent women.

The Tullie Smith House
Is a Glimpse of the Past

A TWO-STORY FRAME house built during the 1830s
is one of the showplaces of Atlanta. It is also on the
National Register of Historic Places. The Tullie Smith
House, now restored to its appearance of the mid-nineteenth
century, is located on the grounds of the Atlanta Historical
Society. The house was acquired in 1969 through the
generosity of banker Mills B. Lane of Atlanta, now of
Savannah, who had it moved to its present site.

Thanks to its wooded setting and the dedicated research
and labor of many knowledgeable volunteers, the house and
its dependencies stand in familiar surroundings. It has been
restored to the point in time when it was considered
"finished," with four main rooms, two shed rooms, a porch
with guestroom at one end, and a detached kitchen
(traditionally separate for protection from fire). It's all freshly
painted, outside a blue-grey with tobacco-brown trim and
inside a sandy-yellow known as "biscuit yellow."

The dependencies include a smokehouse, sarce[1] house, log

---

[1]sarce (sauce) (colloquial): any garden vegetables eaten with meat; often called
"garden sauce."

The Tullie Smith House is a living history lesson

barn, double corncrib, slave cabin and blacksmith shed. The front flower yard is planted with many varieties grown in the nineteenth century. The herb garden abounds in both medicinal and culinary herbs, while the vegetable garden and field crops display samplings of food crops necessary to the family's subsistence.

Its original wooded location in DeKalb County eventually gave way to the encroaching development, and the road in front of the house became known as North Druid Hills Road. The original Smith farm is now Executive Park, with high and mighty buildings.

Miss Tullie Smith (she insisted on being called "Miss") lived in the house many years following her parents' deaths. The house has a fascinating history. Miss Tullie used to tell people she had a firsthand report on the burning of Atlanta by the Yankees. She said her mother told her that *her* mother watched the fire and flames through a window on the second floor of the house. This Grandmother Mason (Mason Mill Road in DeKalb County is named for the family) lived in the house with the Smiths when the Yankees came marching through Georgia.

Miss Tullie claimed that Grandmother Mason saved their valuables when the Yankee raiders stopped by for a visit. "She hid everything under the mattress in her room," said Miss Tullie, "and when she saw the raiders coming, she ran up the steps, jumped into bed and suddenly became very ill, and the raiders looked in and left!"

Miss Tullie was loved by many. Her large frame gave her a statuesque appearance. She always wore large, wide-brimmed hats. She loved flowers and was a "regular" at all the shows, especially during the years when the seasonal events were given at Rich's downtown. She had a great sense of humor, and loved to tell about her favorite description. She was to be speaker at a gathering. The chairman in his introduction said, "Our guest speaker is the second largest thing in DeKalb County. The first is Stone Mountain."

The Tullie Smith House now sits on new ground, but bygone days and customs are relived. Spinning, weaving, quilting and hearth cooking are demonstrated in the house throughout the year. Additional crafts, country music, and animals in the barnyard can be enjoyed during the annual Folklife Festival. The house is warmly welcoming during the Christmas season, decorated with fresh native greenery and berries. Throughout the growing season there are tulips to be exclaimed over, roses to be smelled, cotton bolls bursting, and herbs that conjure up thoughts of savory country stews. For those who are interested in early Atlanta history, the house is open to the public for tours.

Eternal Flame
Snuffed Out

November 28, 1976

THE "ETERNAL FLAME of the Confederacy" has been
snuffed out. Not by the Yankees. By MARTA.

It's gone with the mud around its original setting, at the
northeast corner of Alabama and Whitehall streets.

It had been standing there since 1880 beside the Atlanta
National Building. The building has been torn limb from
limb, or rather floor from floor, by MARTA, which is tearing
up Peachtree. (That section of Whitehall Street has been
renamed Peachtree Street.) The big downtown MARTA
station is the reason why. Where the lamppost stood is now a
swamp of Georgia red mud.

A check with MARTA officials, however, disclosed that it
is really not a lost cause.

"When the building is completely torn down and the
street has been cleared, things will be nice and tidy again,
and we will re-install the lamppost with appropriate
ceremonies," said the man from MARTA. "We have it stored
away for safekeeping. We would not let anything happen to
something as important to the city as the lamppost." [1]

---

[1] The lamppost has been re-installed at the corner of Alabama and South Peachtree
streets.

[163]

Bill Pipkin relights 'The Eternal Flame' at its new location

Well, he is damn right, the lamppost is important to Atlanta! For the benefit of the newcomers here, and for the homefolks who may have forgotten all about the lamppost because they don't come downtown where the action is, here's some background.

The old lamppost was one of fifty that first lighted Atlanta streets on Christmas Eve of 1855. Solomon Luckie was standing by that lamppost when he was fatally injured. After that, the lamppost was kept in the City Hall as a memento of the War Between the States.

In 1880, by resolution of the City Council, it was restored to its original site. Then, in 1919, the United Daughters of the Confederacy, in a drive to mark historic spots in the city, placed a bronze tablet on the post and dedicated it to the memory of General A. J. West, a prominent Atlantan and a Confederate veteran.

In December, 1939, during the festivities of the world premiere of *Gone With the Wind*, the old lamppost was again lighted. Not by the lamplighters with their long tapers, but by none other than the good, old Atlanta Gas Light Company, at a program sponsored by the Old Guard Battalion and the United Daugters of the Confederacy. It was the same day as the big *Gone With the Wind* ball that evening at the City Auditorium.

The light was again termed the Eternal Light of the Confederacy. And as the MARTA man said, "Don't worry, we have it in a safe place. We are taking care of it, and it soon will be re-installed."

And here's an afterthought. There were only two of the gas lampposts left when they were replaced by electric poles. The twin of the downtown post is now at the Atlanta Historical Society. It originally burned in front of the Bell House, an elite men's boarding house from 1878 until after World War II.

The Bell House had many locations during the years, the final one being at the corner of Third and Peachtree streets, now the site of the district office of the J. C. Penney Company. The lamppost was a landmark of the establishment, and in 1951, a group of former residents, who called themselves the Bell House Boys, gave the post to the Atlanta Historical Society.

Yolande's Atlanta

Peachtree Romance

They Came Bearing Gifts

THERE IS A SAYING among the Fourth Estate that there is no such thing as a free lunch. How true it is!

One acquaintance calls at home during the evening. After the usual discussion regarding the weather, I report that I'm getting along fine after an accident (in which I broke my ankle on one side and double-fractured it on the other, resulting in two operations). The caller offers condolences, and then continues, "Now, I want to do something for you, since I didn't know all this. I'll be in town Monday; could you meet me for lunch? I'd love to see you again."

Inasmuch as I have to go to town anyway, I unwillingly accept her invitation. On Monday, as we are finishing our dessert, the waitress brings the bill to the table. My hostess grabs it, saying, "This is on me." When I suggest we go Dutch, she says, "Certainly not! This is a luncheon gift to you, as I didn't know of your operation."

Digging into her purse for the money, she says, "Don't worry, I stopped by the bank on the way down."

As we leave, she says, "This has been more fun. Let's do it again soon. Oh, just to help you I thought I'd bring along the announcement of my daughter's engagement. I'd love for it

to be in the Sunday paper. Do you think it could be at the top of the first page? It would mean so much to her. Of course, *I* don't mind where it appears, but she wants to send the paper to her future in-laws. Do you think you could?"

The mother dashes into the office. "Oh, I'm so glad you are here! I was thinking of you yesterday and I bought this cute potholder at the church bazaar. I saw it with its red trim and I knew it was for you. I must run now, but I'll call later this week to tell you the great news. My daughter is getting married!"

Holidays are made to order for mothers of the brides who wish to pave the way for announcements of their daughters' engagements. Flowers arrive at both home and office. Boxes of candy, especially at St. Valentine's Day, arrive with brief notes such as, "Have a happy day! I've been missing you! We must get together soon! Love from us both."

The engagement announcement arrives soon afterwards with a card saying, "Here's my daughter's engagement for Sunday. Thanks so much. P.S. Hope the flowers are still in bloom," or "Hope you enjoyed the candy."

Here's another case, except the father drops by the office, with an obvious package (which must be a bottle of bourbon). "I was coming by the advertising department to check on my company's ad, and my wife asked me to bring this to you. I know it's the brand you like!" Then out he goes.

In a few weeks the wife calls, "Well," she says in a breathless voice, "I had no idea I'd be calling you about this. My daughter is getting married! I know your hands are full now, but could you possibly squeeze this announcement in next Sunday's paper?" (Sunday space is filled for a month ahead.)

She comes into the society department with a halting walk. In a quiet voice she asks, "Are you Miss Gwin?"

"That's Miss Gwin at the desk in the corner," replies my associate.

The woman comes over and sits down. In a soft voice she says, "My daughter is getting married and I'm at a loss as to what to do. I had no idea she was in love, and she told us last night. Will you please tell me what to do now, and will you write up the engagement for me? I'm in shock and I just can't do it myself. My husband is in the same condition, and he left town this morning to go fishing."

After a brief talk with her, in which I advise her what to do about the announcement for the paper, she tells me she will come by to see me later.

Then, after fumbling in her bag, she brings out a green paper bag.

"I stopped by Rich's on my way here, and I saw this little gift, and decided I'd bring it to you. It's just a thought, and don't worry about writing me a thank-you note."

Arriving home from work late one winter evening, I did the natural thing. I stopped at the mailbox, hoping for some checks and invitations, instead of bills.

There were some nice letters from friends. Also a box, a medium-sized cracker box, wrapped in foil and trimmed with a red ribbon. It's too late for Christmas and too early for my birthday.

Once inside the house, the mystery unfurls like a flag. The note reads, "Here's a box of that great fudge I make with Pet Milk. I had my bridge club here today and I made the fudge for us to nibble on. I just made some for you as I know you are a chocolate nut like me. I'll see you soon."

Soon? I hardly knew her. A mere speaking acquaintance. But the clues were there. *She has a daughter getting married.* True. Soon the announcement arrives with a note, "I'm going to be bringing you some more fudge real soon."

Heed Those Bridal Superstitions

June 7, 1970

THE MARCH TO THE ALTAR is in full swing now that it is June. Churches are booked to capacity, and marriages are being performed almost on an hourly—and sometimes half-hourly—schedule.

With all the flurry of planning and trousseau shopping finished, and most of the parties already happy memories, superstitions, like so many monsters, begin to creep into the picture.

Really, it's an old bridal custom to be superstitious. All brides know they must wear something old, something new, something borrowed and something blue.

Then there is the day—Monday for health; Tuesday for wealth; Wednesday, the best day of all; Thursday for crosses; Friday for losses; and Saturday, no luck at all!

Brides had better pay heed to the *Dont's*!

Don't wear green. It is the color of the fairies, and evil spirits will haunt you.

Don't sign your name on your wedding day until you become a bride.

Don't see the bridegroom before the ceremony.

Don't break anything, especially a mirror.

Don't look into your mirror on your wedding day unless you add something to your toilette, even if it is just a dab of powder on the nose.

Don't weep, but shed a few tears for good luck.

Don't leave the church by a different door than the one you entered.

Don't have a double wedding; it means unhappiness for one couple.

Don't forget to step over the church sill with your right foot to insure happiness.

Another superstition which for years has been followed is the one about not trying on the entire wedding costume until time to leave home for the church.

This does not hold too well now. Very few brides dress at home anymore. They dress at the church.

Now a few final notes for the bride.

Questions are always asked about thank-you notes for the wedding gifts.

Social custom calls for the bride to write a note as soon as a wedding gift arrives. Few brides these days, with all the rushing around that they do before the marriage, have the time or the strength to sit down and write a note, much less one that would be gracious and appreciative.

It is perfectly proper for a bride to write her notes when she returns from her wedding trip.

If a bride is intent on doing the right thing, she can send cards which read, "This is to acknowledge that your wedding gift has been received. A note of appreciation and thanks will be forthcoming."

It is nice to know that your gift, whether a potato masher or a silver service, has at least been delivered, but nine times out of ten that receipt card is all you'll ever get from the bride.

Now, a few words about the wedding cake.

Ever notice that the bride and bridegroom eat only the first piece of cake?

Don't worry, some kind soul is always alerted to remove the top tier, wrap it and have it stored in someone's freezer so that the bride and groom can enjoy it on their first anniversary.

If there is no freezer available, the cake may be wrapped in a brandy-soaked cloth and stored in an airtight container.

You don't have to have a miniature bride and bridegroom on the top layer. You don't have to have wedding bells. You can have flowers made of icing or you can have fresh pastel flowers. Remember, it's your wedding cake; your father is paying for it, and you can have it made your way even though it may crumble your caterer's dream. One Atlanta girl had a candy plane on her cake, for the bridegroom was in the Air Force.

If you are an unmarried guest at the wedding reception, be sure to take a piece of the cake home and place it under your pillow to sleep on for three nights. The third night you are supposed to dream of the man you will marry.

Who says superstitions are just for the bride?

My Daughter Is Getting Married

THE SHOT HEARD 'round the world in the Revolutionary War was a mere whimper compared to the wail of mothers who say, "My daughter is getting married!"

The mother is thrust into another orbit; her emotions go haywire, her personality changes, and often her blood pressure hits its highest mark. Aspirins are her standby (thankfully, not wine or bourbon), and her opening statement in every phone call is, "I'm about to lose my mind and I'm on my third bottle of aspirin. If I can make it to the wedding, it will be a miracle!"

That magic phrase of five little words, "My daughter is getting married," has many facets.

THE GLEEFUL: "Thank goodness she will have a husband and, I hope, children."

THE FRANTIC: "I'm going crazy! I don't know what to do first! What about my dress for the wedding? And I'll have to get a permanent right away. And, oh, the reception, the invitations, the guest list. And, oh, I'll have to engage the church. Oh, my heavens! What does a mother do?"

THE DOUBTFUL: "Oh, has she made the right choice of a husband? Will he make her happy? Is his family background as good as ours? I must call the paper. Do you suppose we can have the top spot at the top of the page? Oh, I hope Jim will let me have new draperies in the living and dining rooms. . . ." (She must keep up with the Joneses in staging the wedding.)

Aside from her frantic antics, a mother with a daughter getting married becomes a publicity pest as things progress along the bridal path. These pests, not unlike wasps and hornets, tend to strike at random and without warning. Here are a few examples:

INVITATIONS: An invitation usually arrives ten days to two weeks before the affair. The week of the party the expected phone call comes. "We do hope you are coming to our party. Would it be asking too much of you to put it in your social column? It would be so nice, as we are announcing our daughter's engagement at the party. It's so exciting to her to have the news in the paper. We are crazy about the young man. I'll send you the formal announcement in a few days. Do put it in the paper, the first Sunday available that you can give her a nice write-up."

An invitation is received from a hostess unknown to me. She wants me to meet some bridge and sewing-group friends. "Just an informal get-together for luncheon," she writes on the invitation. There is also the usual "Please reply" on the lower left-hand corner of the card or invitation. The date of the "informal gathering" is in two weeks. Attempting to postpone the "Please reply" until I can identify the hostess, I reach a dead end. So I reply, "Sorry, unable to attend."

Then she calls. "Now, don't tell me you are not coming!

All of us want to see you! Most of all, my daughter will be home from college for the summer, and I do want you to meet her and get to know her. . . ."

That was the clue! Six months later, the mother-hostess has another party. "My daughter is getting married, and you just *must* come to meet her fiancé! This will be the first of many parties, and I'll send items to you, so let's keep in touch."

THE MOTHER-DAUGHTER CONSPIRACY: They pop into the office. "Surprise!" chimes the mother. "We came by on our way to Rich's for some shopping. My daughter, here, wants so much to meet you. Can you join us for lunch?"

Upon my declining, she says, "We'll see you again soon. I have a great secret to tell you!" It was as obvious as handwriting on the mirror.

FLATTERY: Seeing me at a cocktail party inspires the usual build-up. "Oh," she gushes, "I haven't seen you in ages. You look *great*, and I love the way you are wearing your hair. It's so becoming!"

Later during the party, the expected happens. She slithers up again. "I just happened to think, let's have lunch one day next week and catch up on the news and gossip. I've always wanted to really know you better."

After several refusals of her invitation, I am besieged with phone calls "just to check on me." She says she has heard about my accident. I think, however, that her interest extends beyond my health. And now I know. The mother sends in her daughter's engagement with a note reading, "I need your advice on what to do about this upcoming wedding. Will you meet me for lunch today?"

A mere acquaintance hovers around me at a party. The

pattern is the same. "Don't you look grand! I'm so glad to see you again. It's been ages! Here, let my husband get you a refill. What have you been doing, except working, of course? I read all your articles. Do you know that we've just moved into our new home? We just love it. Oh, we built it—just like we wanted to. You *must* come out to see us."

About that time her husband returns with my drink, saying, "Gosh, you should wear that combination of beige and red all the time. You look great. Can I get you something from the buffet table?"

I know the usual is on the way. The mother continues, "It is great seeing you. Don't forget to come to see us. I'll be calling you real soon to tell you about all the grand plans we have. My daughter is getting married and I want to write it up."

FORTHRIGHTNESS: The mother backs me into a corner for the blow.

"You haven't forgotten or lost my daughter's engagement, have you? I'll send you another one, but keep this in mind, do give her a top spot in the Sunday paper—not daily, but Sunday. We have relatives all over the state who take only the Sunday paper. Of course, it doesn't matter to me, but I know my daughter wants a nice top-billing of her wedding for her scrapbook. Anyway, the upper left-hand corner on the first page would be nice. I have always heard that people read from left to right through the paper. Could you save me about fifty extra copies for my relatives?" Only the need of another drink at the bar provides an escape.

Even now, the "smelling salts period" goes on, for women are still wailing and whispering as they make a phone call to announce in hushed tones, "My daughter is getting married!"

A Few of the
Fifty-Seven Varieties

MANY LETTERS included here arrived during the period when the long engagement and wedding stories with pictures were used.

It is very important that I point out that there are many, many mothers who are level-headed and on their toes. Nor do my many friends and acquaintances fit into the following categories. They call or write without fuss and frills, and give me the Great News. Daughter or Sonny Boy is getting married, can you . . . ?

But then, as now, there are mothers sitting on the panic button. The following are what we at the paper call (thanks to Heinz) "the fifty-seven varieties."

THE NAME-DROPPERS: "You know, Miss Gwin, my husband is a good friend of your publisher, and I'm sure he (the publisher) would want our daughter to have the best place and the best write-up. I don't mean to be a name-dropper, but I thought I would mention this to you."

"Dear Miss Gwin, Enclosed is my daughter's engagement for next Sunday's paper. (The paper requires engagement announcements a month in advance.) It's important that it be in that day as there is a party to celebrate the event Saturday. The party will be given by our friends at the Piedmont Driving Club.

"That will explain the importance of the affair. We are not members of the club, but our friends are.

"I'm enclosing the write-up for your paper, plus a picture of my daughter and her fiancé. I insist that both be used. We have important connections in the city. We know the governor. I'm a member of the DAR. The bridegroom was a member of an important fraternity at the University of Georgia and was an outstanding student.

"Our daughter is our only girl child and was president of her sorority.

"These facts should impress you, and I'm expecting as well as *demanding* a good story. They are marrying in June and I'll want their picture leaving the church in the newspaper. My husband will be getting in touch with you later."

THE SNOB: The mother writes to the head man, "I feel sure that with your position you can get my daughter's engagement in the paper on the date I request.

"I don't have the time to waste on discussing the story with your staff members. Orders from you will be enough. You know our position in society and my husband's high-ranking title plus our social club membership."

THE RELIGIOUS ROUTE: Mothers have gone so far as to ask their ministers to (1) write a reference on the character of the future bride and her involvement in church activities, or (2) send the engagement in with a note saying, "This lovely young girl has fallen in love with a fine young man, and they have my blessings. I hope you will give them a nice write-up at the top of the page."

THE NOT-SURE-OF-HERSELF MOTHER: Her requests run like this, "My daughter's engagement is enclosed. I want to emphasize the fact that her grandparents and great-grandparents were original Atlanta pioneers, builders of our great city, and highly prominent in social and business circles. Our name is linked with all important groups in the city like the Arts, Symphony and charities. For these reasons, my daughter deserves special attention."

Another not-so-sure-of-herself mother goes about it this way: She has her husband write to someone in the executive office of the paper. The letter, passed on to me, reads in part, "Hi, ole buddy, missed seeing you on the golf course during the weekend. You doing O.K.?

"Can you pass on the enclosed to the society editor with a little urging to give it special attention? She is our first daughter to marry and, of course, we want the best for her.

"Thanks, pal, see you soon at one of our various club luncheons."

That Daughter of Mine

HERE'S A MOTHER who has been in the planning stage since her daughter entered high school. It begins the first year.

She calls, "I am so thrilled—that daughter of mine has been asked to join a sorority! My husband and I and our daughter are going to the mountains for the weekend and I am hoping you will put in a little item that we will be visiting my sister and that my daughter is a new member of the sorority."

Years pass with other requests, such as, "Can you believe this? Our daughter has been invited to attend some frat parties at the University of Georgia. She'd be thrilled to have it in your column, if you could possibly squeeze it in on Sunday. She can put it in her scrapbook."

Daughter is graduating from high school. The call comes again.

"I'm so proud of my child I don't know what to do. Can you believe she is graduating and has been chosen to be in the May Day Court? If you will use some of this news about the queen and her court, I'd be glad to send you the information."

Several months later daughter is going to college.

Another call comes from mother, "Are you listing the names of the college-bound girls? Well, that daughter of mine is one of them. I'm *so* proud!"

For four years calls come about "that daughter of mine" coming home for the various holidays during the school year.

Then, a year later, the bombshell explodes.

"Well," she begins with heavy breathing, "this is me again. I know you get tired of my calling, but this time it is the most exciting of all. *She is getting married!* I'm so excited and thrilled that I'm out of my mind—I don't know what to do first! But *please* save a nice spot at the top of the society page, the first page, you know, for her write-up and pictures. I'm in such a dither now that I'll have to get my husband's secretary to send it in. And don't forget we want you to come to the wedding and reception."

The next day I receive a box of candy from you-know-who with a note reading, "You've been so great during the past years. *Please* give my daughter the *best* spot in the paper. A Sunday, of course. I'll keep in touch. P.S. I knew you *loved* chocolate."

We Should Have Done Better!

WHEN I BEGAN getting lots of letters—and did I get letters!—for a few minutes I thought it was fan mail. However, the thrill vanished as the contents unfolded, as some of the following specimens will show.

"This is my daughter's engagement. I don't want *one word* cut out, as I composed it myself. I am a college graduate, and I know words and how to spell them. If you *do* have the acid gall to cut this, I'll report you to the editor." (Little did she know I was the editor!)

From a bride, "I want to have an explanation of why you won't use the picture of me and my fiancé. The groom is a very important part of a wedding. . . .

"My home town paper used both of us, so why do you and your paper act so uppity?

"If I have to have my picture made, it will be extra expense and inconvenience to me, thanks to your dumb rules."

Another bride writes, "I want to complain about my engagement write-up. My fiancé's picture was blocked out. We both wanted to announce our plans to marry. We are *two* people and are equal as persons and children of God. We both are getting married. We both should be considered and treated equally in your paper. We don't want a routine write-up. It seems to me your paper could be polite enough to grant a request by a subscriber."

"I want this announcement in the Sunday paper, not the daily. I only take the Sunday paper, just as all my friends do, and business associates only take the Sunday paper and I want them to read it.

"My cousins are going to send the announcement in, as my parents are dead. One of my cousins has an aunt who works there, and I have been working myself for fifteen years and know exactly what I am doing, so don't bother to send one of those silly identification cards to me. Just call my cousin's aunt. You have mighty crazy rules to be as big as you are. . . ."

"Dear Miss Gwin:

"My daughter is getting married next Sunday. The wedding will be consummated on the front lawn of the church. . . . Please send a photographer. . . ."

"I am sending in the announcement of my daughter's wedding. She and her fiancé have my sincere blessing. . . ."

"Dear Miss Gwin:

"I received your card to sign and verify the engagement of my daughter. I am returning it unsigned. My husband and I oppose her marrying this man. He is seven years older, is divorced, and has a two-year-old child.

"If she sends it in, don't print it. We have told our lawyer, and we are prepared to sue the paper if you publish it. . . ."

"I sent in my son's engagement, as the girl doesn't live here. What made you send me that verification card? Did you think I was lying? I just want you to know I tore up the card and you can do the same thing with the announcement. Just forget it."

"I am sending in my daughter's engagement. Please don't cut anything out because it will look very skimpy in her scrapbook.

"We will be glad to pay for the extra space. We want the names of the grandparents included, because they, as we, have been subscribers for many, many years. Please call me and tell me the price and I'll send you a check by return mail."

"You have to have rules, I know, but why are you so highhanded in telling people what to do about their own daughter's engagement? Why can't she have a picture for her engagement as well as for her wedding?"

(The *Atlanta Journal* had printed rules regarding engagement and wedding announcements. The rules were mailed upon request. In the fifties, sixties and part of the seventies, the *Atlanta Journal* used only one picture.)

She continued, "I do not agree with you, and I protest your high-and-mighty attitude. Why not be generous? Why does the public, like me, have to abide by your stinking rule that some dumbbell made up! Your readers and subscribers should have the say-so when the information concerns them. You should see how nice our home town paper is—pictures and long, lovely descriptions. Our paper has very little income. Yours has much, much more. So you should do better!"

How to Know When You're Getting the Brushoff

"**B**UT HE SAID he loved me!" wailed the young girl. "Me? I just charged it up to experience," drawled the mature woman.

"He's not the only pebble on the beach," snapped the siren. "The dear boy, I must have failed somewhere to make him change," said the meek little maid.

Women often break their engagements, and have darn good reasons for doing so. Somehow, the masculine brushoff smacks of more originality, more varied excuses, and sometimes more humor, than the feminine brushoff.

How do they tell the girl of their dreams that the flame of love has turned to ashes? That "that old feeling" is just a song after all? So, what's your line, men? Here are some excuses, as spoken by certain types.

THE MARTYR: "Darling, you're the most wonderful woman in the world. Please, before we part, believe me when I say that I shall carry your image in my heart always. I shall go to my grave knowing that only you could have made me happy, only you could I have loved. But, alas, marriage is not for us."

THE PLAYBOY: "There will never be a party girl like you, for you and only you make me feel important when we go out. You are fascinating, delightful; we can go everywhere, dance under the stars, love, and be happy. But, darling, this party life is not for you. You would be bored to death. You should lead a more solid, routine life, have a fine husband, a wonderful home and family. I'm the party type, dear, and I shall think of you in years to come as a real party pal. Don't ever forget me—think of me as I come home to an empty apartment while you and your lovely family are together around a festive dinner table, or before the fire on Christmas Eve."

THE MARRIED MAN: "I have dreaded this moment when I must bare my heart and soul to you. You have made me forget my unhappiness for many wonderful months. My happiness has been in your every word, in being with you, but I knew that it was stolen paradise. I feel that I've been a cad, but she needs me now more than ever. But remember, she is my wife in name only. You will always be the one love of my life. You do understand me, don't you? This must be farewell, but never goodbye. You shall be with me always—in my thoughts."

THE DIVORCED MAN: "I have made a mess of one marriage and I can't make a second one. I can't ruin your wonderful life as I did Annabelle's, for I know now that I bring only unhappiness to women. I am doomed to a life of loneliness. I cannot ask another woman to gamble on marriage with me."

THE AMBITIOUS MAN: "I love you too much to ask you to struggle with me during these lean years. It is not fair to you. You deserve the best, and I cannot give you the best—now. In the future, yes. But it is unfair to ask you to wait for me while I make the money to take care of such a wonderful woman."

THE SUMMER BACHELOR: "You've made my summer a dream come true. It has been the light in a dark and gloomy life. To think we have to part, now that we have found each other, is breaking my heart. This has been the happiest summer of my life. How I envy those men in your home town who can date you this year! I'll count the days until next summer when we can be together again."

THE MOTHER COMPLEX: "I know you can understand that I could never ask you to take second place in my heart. My mother has held first place always. You are too fine to be other than a man's first love. Fate brought us together but, cruel that she is, she has separated us."

THE ATTENTION-WITHOUT-INTENTION TYPE: He sidesteps matrimony with "big brother" behavior, and the let's-be-pals attitude which may continue for years with wedding bells ringing on deaf ears. (On the other hand, a friendship between a man and woman is an entirely different story and is a rare and wonderful relationship. If it's genuine, it will survive many marriages.)

THE HURT BRUSHOFF: Something the girl of his dreams has said or done has hurt him so much he has had to fade out of her life. He just can't take it. Of course, he never admits what the "hurt" has been.

COLLEGE-SWEETHEART-IN-TOWN: (She never meant anything to him, though.) It's a good excuse for a quick exit. Jealousy is another weapon. "I can't bear to be out with you and see other men holding you close when dancing, or lighting your cigarette, or buying you a drink," is his line.

INSTANT BRUSHOFFS: Like coffee, tea and soup, there are several. Foremost among them is, "As soon as I land, I'll write," or "Don't call me, I'll call you." But by far the best is the frank and earnest method; as the doctors would say, a clean cut. "Florabelle, I must confess, I just don't love you any more and can't marry you!"

When these symptoms are noticed, a girl had better make another date for Saturday night, and quickly. Lover boy has bit the dust, and it's a case of, "Weep no more, my lady."

Flame Flickers?
Douse It!

November 1, 1959

HOW DO YOU forget a man?
You don't.

Well, then, how do you break an engagement or tell him you don't love him any more?

There are many ways, and feminine intuition being what it is, the road to the breaking point is long and winding—and often interesting.

Some women break their engagements in a cool, hard, indifferent manner. Some try to be sweet and tender and drippy about the whole thing and shed bitter tears. (That's silly. Why let him see you for the last time with a red, running nose and swollen eyes?)

Others are dramatic and try to out-Bankhead Darling Tallulah. Some try to be honest with themselves, as well as with the man, and are sincere in their farewell address.

Then the really clever ones see the handwriting on the wall even through the rosy hue of romance and break off first. ("I know we both feel the same, Archibald, that this whole thing has been a mistake.")

Some are inconsiderate and write him a note from their honeymoon with someone else. ("Maurice and I found each other—our love is bigger than both of us, but I shall love you always.")

A recent article listed excuses for the masculine brushoff, given as the boyfriend found the fires of love flickering out. The following are the feminine counterparts.

THE CAREER GIRL: "I've always worked and made my own money and done pretty much as I please; I'm independent now. A wife, though, must be dependent upon a man. I don't think I could be. I could never let a man overshadow me. That's why, darling, our marriage could never be—superiority is inborn in me. I know you must understand, because of your wonderful, superior nature."

THE WIDOW: "Your companionship has been marvelous. It has been the nearest thing to perfect happiness since dear Rollo left me. But I am not the one for you. You need someone who will be all yours. Part of me still belongs to Rollo. I am afraid for you, dear, that life with me would not measure up to your dreams. But I shall always be your friend."

THE DIVORCÉE: "Of course, you must know that Alfonso and I got a friendly divorce. It should be that way, you know. Actually, we are the best of friends and always will be. You know how it is—we will have dates now and then and we will dine together at our separate homes. I do not think that you, with your sense of propriety and your reserved manner, would approve. You would be too jealous and our marriage would go on the rocks."

ANOTHER DIVORCÉE: "What can I offer you, darling? My life with Sebastian was hell on earth and it was all my fault, too. I am not the type to be a married woman.

Sebastian can vouch for this, but I know that you would not bring yourself to ask him. Some people are just not the type to be married. I am like that. But you, dear, should be married. You will make some girl a wonderful husband and I'll do all I can to help you find her."

THE PAST-FORTY: "Our friendship is one of the most wonderful things in my life. I don't think I could have met the issues or won the battles without you at my side. But I know that you are tired of being a one-man service league. I have no initiative without you at my side. I would be a drag on you always. I'd be the real ball and chain around your neck. You need someone who is your companion, friend, lover, and wife all rolled into one. I don't think I could offer you the inspiration you deserve."

JUST ANY WOMAN: "I just must be truthful with you, Marcel. I have tried to fall in love with you for a long time. I *do* love you in a way, like I love ice cream sodas, blue underwear, mad hats, black stockings and red shoes, but I can't love you like a wife. I have tried and it is hopeless. But remember, I shall love you as a friend."

THE DEBUTANTE: "Oh, this wonderful, gay life! I love every minute. The days are not long enough. Let's not be serious now, Philbert—we have the future ahead of us to plan many things. Let's live now!"

The brushoffs are endless, if you are the explaining type. But there are easier ways. Don't be at home when he calls. Or, if you do answer the phone, say, "Let me call you back, Ezra, there's company here, and I do want to talk to you." Then don't call back. Or don't answer letters. Tell him you are dated up until the Fourth of July and then you just may go to the mountains.

Write him a note—but don't make it overly sentimental and mushy. It could land on page one of the paper, you know. Postpone the wedding date. Keep on postponing it. Take a long trip and don't write. Get a job in another town. Tell him that there's poverty in the family, that you have an incurable disease, that you are a spendthrift, an alcoholic, and are jealous.

Of course, if all else fails, you can always tell the man, "I saw you last night and did not get that old feeling!"

That is, of course, if he is still around or hasn't given you the brushoff.

Being a Wallflower Has Its Advantages

November 29, 1959

BEING A WALLFLOWER has its advantages—sometimes.

Of course, if your new shoes are too small, and pinch, it's a downright blessing in disguise.

According to powder room gossip, the way some men dance has ended more romances than moonlight nights and fireside chats have promoted.

Holding a man is one thing, but the way he holds you on the dance floor is another.

These men are known as the ballroom bores.

They never ask you to sit this one out.

They never suggest a stroll on the terrace to look at the moon or smoke a cigarette. Oh, no. They want to dance every dance. "We came to dance, didn't we?" is their slogan. It doesn't matter whether it's a waltz, a tango, jitterbug, rumba or the samba. It's dance, boy, dance!

Here's a rundown on some of the worst.

OUT OF HAND TYPE: This is the one who lets his hand roam all over the girl's hips in tempo with the music. Rhythm, boy, rhythm.

CORSAGE CRUSHER: One whirl around the dance floor with this character and your flowers look like they have been pressed in the family album since the Spanish-American War. He won't listen to your plea that holding you so tight will crush the flowers. "I want to hold you close," he whispers.

SNUGGLE BUG: Hugging and snuggling before all those people right on the dance floor? It is not only embarrassing to the girl whose real heartthrob is watching from the sidelines, but there are better places to snuggle up a little closer!

JERK: The dance teachers know all the latest steps, but this guy knows some better ones. He will combine waltz steps with those of the Apache dancer and suddenly does a drop kick with Georgia Tech precision.

SKIRT SCOUT: Better wear your prettiest and fanciest petticoat with this guy. When he dances he clutches your skirt, pulls it up like a curtain. He is really not to blame—he just doesn't know any better.

KISS IN THE DARK: Usually repulsive. Bad for morale and makeup.

FLAME THROWER: He may set the world on fire with his charms, but he is more apt to set your hair and your clothes on fire with his dangling cigarette.

MOTHER'S BOY: Here's one who likes to dance away the hours with his head on your soft, white, swanlike throat.

SQUEEZER: He thinks he is doing you a favor hugging you and whispering sweet nothings in your ear and murmuring things like, "If I could hold you close like this always, I would be happy."

PLAYBOY: He holds you ever so tenderly. He keeps you in one corner—usually the darkest one—and kisses your hand when the dance is over. And says, "To think you let me, of all men here, have this dance with you. I shall be forever grateful for giving me just these brief moments." He never dances with you again.

The doom which once surrounded the position of being "a wallflower" suddenly becomes a colorful rainbow.

The sidelines are like an oasis on the sand-swept deserts of life. It's like home and mother after a journey's end.

But here again is a problem. How to get rid of the dance bores? Excuses can be anything from playing deaf to "Let's dance the next one!" Or you could let your petticoat fall to the floor, break the heel off your shoe, announce that you have poison ivy, or make a sudden exit to check on the parking meter. When all else fails, you can either faint or turn on the fire alarm.

Personal Memos on Calling Cards Are Dangerous

December 7, 1941

NEXT TIME YOU WANT to dash off a memo to yourself, don't use the back of your visiting card just because it is handy in your bag.

After all, visiting cards are really for calling purposes. They are not to be used as memo pads to carry such intimate notations as "get some peach-colored step-ins and see if girdles have come in," or such everyday matters as "two pounds of lamb chops, coffee, three dozen oranges."

A variety of notes, messages and shopping lists scribbled on the backs of visiting cards have landed on silver trays during the past weeks, as guests have unconsciously dropped their cards at debut parties, happily unaware that their secrets have caused untold merriment to the hosts.

In checking over calling cards left at their parties, Atlanta hostesses have found shopping and grocery lists, telephone numbers, drawings, personal notations and professional cards.

For some reason, guests—apparently a majority of them—dip into their bags, slip cards out of their cases and drop them into the card tray, without so much as a glance at the backs to see what they may have jotted down on them.

Here are some samples of "back notes" collected at random from Atlanta hostesses.

"See about the laundry and check with the diaper service. Think six dozen will do for Junior."

"Call Dearborn 1869 and ask for Tom. He is darling."

"Call Mrs. Gresham for flowers for the cemetery; borrow the black gown from Mary; buy the cocktail glasses; get price on rum and gin. Then check for bourbon per case."

"Ask John to change the date to Sunday. Accept Mrs. Harmon's invitation; check on the cute lieutenant from Fort McPherson; ask Sallie Cobb about the other date for her debut dance."

"Ask Wilson for dinner Friday. Order ice cream."

"Draw $20 from the bank, and don't forget to hide the bank book in the coffee urn tonight after the late news broadcast."

"Call the Buckhead Taxi Service and check about Saturday night."

Messages written on the back of cards and passed around at dinner parties reveal some interesting thoughts. For instance: "You are the most beautiful girl at this table. May you be my dinner partner for life?"

"What do you think of the speaker? Isn't she a dull number? How long do you think we will have to stay here? She can talk but she can't speak! Dull as dishwater! I'd be happier if I were in jail! Never again!"

Sometimes writers jot down the toasts they plan to give. For example, "Here is to the land we love and the love we land."

"Here's to your teeth; if you will be true to them, they will never be false to you!"

"Here's to clocks and men, the former to tell us time, and the latter to help us pass it away!"

At one of the largest parties of the season, one hostess found this interesting list on the back of the card of a well-known Atlantan. "Ice cream soda, 15¢; car tokens, 15¢; *Time* and *Life*, 25¢; blue garters, 10¢; half a yard of pale pink and blue ribbon, 8¢; cleansing tissue, 10¢; bobby pins, 10¢; chewing gum, 5¢; gum drops, 10¢; stockings, $1.95; gloves, $1.95; girdle, $3.95; 2 gallons of gas, 44¢; another ice cream soda, 15¢; total, $8.62; $1.38 left for the rest of the week."

In addition to personal visiting cards, a number of Atlanta hostesses have found in their card trays the cards of well-known business firms or other establishments. These cards, previously slipped into card cases, have been slipped into the trays by mistake, and sometimes, because the guest does not have one of her own. Cards have shown up from a number of well-known lawyers, florists, clerks in various department stores, and even one from a detective agency.

Before car tokens were used, many hostesses recalled finding car tickets among the cards left, and one time there were some transfers slipped among the cards.

So remember, if you have any notes to be included among your souvenirs, buy yourself a notebook and pencil to carry around with you, and don't dash off notes on your calling cards. It may be embarrassing to you later. An example: one young lady denied her engagement to a certain young man, then left her card with the following notations, "See about decorations for the altar. Order the invitations. See about bridesmaids' dresses. Get the license at the courthouse at ten o'clock."

It Is the Finish Line
That Counts!

SCHUBERT'S UNFINISHED Symphony seems out of tune in comparison to Society's Unfinished Cocktail Sentences.

A cocktail party, in today's lingo, is a happening.

That means anything can happen and often does.

Once upon a time an Atlanta girl and her parents gave a big cocktail party at their home. Long before the bar closed, daughter and her beau were married in the living room. All the guests stood around awestruck, but attentive, clutching their highball glasses, as the minister intoned, "Dearly beloved, we are gathered together. . . ."

That was quite a happening.

If cocktail conversation could be recorded, the finished product would be received with mixed reaction or emotion. Happenings of this sort could be disastrous; lawsuits could be forthcoming, divorces begun, friends lost and reputations ruined.

But it is the unfinished bits of conversation which intrigue, excite, and provide the element of mystery.

Suppose, then, you were in the maddening cocktail crowd

and hear a woman say, "I was there just a minute, so I asked him if his kidneys were good, and. . . ."

A man at a recent party left some listeners rigid with fear when he said, "I left her hanging from a ledge, but. . . ."

Or the woman who caused wonderment among a group when she said, "I was in bed and I saw the doorknob turn. . . ."

Mystery hit an all-time high when a woman whispered to another, "She's got everything—family, money, beauty, lovely home—but. . . ."

Gossip flies with the speed of a jet at cocktail parties. It is much better when a comment is iced with spice.

"If she has any sense at all, and gets a good lawyer, she can skin him of every dime he has, rather than let that woman have him," is a good example.

Or this one, "I hope that widow does get him, because he has been a good husband and father, and his wife has been a real. . . ."

Things like the following are unnerving, to say the least. "It takes only a few drops to kill, but less will. . . ."

"She *says* she is going alone, but you know what happened when she said that last year and. . . ."

"I suppose you *know* why she is wearing that special dress. . . ."

"The setting was perfect, with an open window on the nineteenth floor right at the back. . . ."

The anticipation of a big game hunt in Africa dimmed as some guests heard a woman say, "Now, upstairs under the bed there is. . . ."

It is hard to keep from choking on your drink when someone drifts by and you hear something like, "I looked around and there was this huge butcher knife, so. . . ."

Bits like, "I know it is true because my son-in-law's stepmother's aunt said her cousin told her," or "Did you hear just why they are giving this party? Well, his mother said. . . ." can cause sleepless nights.

The cocktail-party status seekers—they are the ones who will stand with just the right people in order to be seen by the other right people, naturally—seldom talk. Some of them are sly, little foxes and want to listen and add to their name-dropping vocabulary. The half-finished sentences drift over their heads like so much smoke.

It is the fun people who can manage to enjoy themselves and wonder about other people and what they say and what they hear.

"Three A.M. will be the best time, then nobody will know that. . . ." Someone says, while someone else will gulp and drink and say, "Next time they pass the chicken livers, ask the maid; I'll bet she will tell you the real truth or she will tell you. . . ."

At one party there was almost a mass exit of guests bent on a mercy mission when one man, busy dipping shrimp in a gooey sauce, said, "It was just a few minutes ago, and he went down for the third time, and. . . ."

Want to Ruin a Good Aria? Check This List for Ideas!

April 21, 1961

THE MOST POPULAR question in some circles these days is, "Of course, you're going to the opera?"

And nine times out of ten, whether a person is going or not, the answer is the same, "Yes, I can hardly wait! Isn't it all too thrilling and exciting? You *must* see my dress for *La Boheme!*"

But not I. I answer, "I hope not. There's no pest control."

"Pests! Are you crazy? The Fox Theater is all spick-and-span for the season," says someone.

No. Not crazy. There are *people pests* and opera week is their open season.

Here's a quick rundown on the more common varieties.

THE CLAPPERS: They start to applaud the instant one of the singers stops to take a deep breath, or when the aria is half over.

THE WHISPERERS: These are of two classes. One is the woman trying to explain the story of the opera to her husband (or date), with such enlightening bits of information as, "Now, in this next scene the tenor is supposed to leave, and when he does the baritone will come in and make love to the soprano. . . ."

The other type is the gossip whisperer. "Just look over there at Honeysuckle Cornpone. I'll bet she had that dress sent out on approval. You know Ferdinand couldn't afford it. They are in debt up to *here!* And look at who's got a date with the dark Russian! Bet she bought his ticket. If we walk out during intermission she's sure to avoid us!"

THE NAME DROPPERS: They announce to all in sitting and hearing distance who everybody is, whether they know them or not. They also let everybody around know that they have been to opera in New York, Milan, and Paris.

THE LATECOMERS: They will always be with us, and will always be disturbing.

THE BAGGERS: Women, of course. They drop their bags and cause a mad scramble to locate lipsticks, compacts, car keys, etc.

LITTLE MISS FIX-ITS: They have done their makeup tricks at home, but there is something about a public appearance that inspires an encore. They raise their arms to check their hairdos, sometimes even combing them. They do a repair job on their makeup. They take their coats or furs off, and then put them on again.

THE WHISTLERS: They think they add spirit and enthusiasm to the applause.

THE AISLE HOPPERS: Up and down the aisle they go, to speak here and there. The result is always the same—lights go out and they become lost.

THE REFRESHMENT SEEKERS: They always bring their candy, popcorn, etc., plus a paper cup of some liquid, back into the theater after intermission.

Pests? They are all over the place. It's hard enough to cope with them in everyday routine things, but to have to take them at the opera, when you're all dressed up and hardly able to breathe in your new girdle and tight shoes. . . .

It's home and Perry Como for me. If there are any pests with him, a flip of the switch and it's all over.

Tea Dances Out of Step on Social Scene

September 26, 1971

W HAT HAS HAPPENED to the tea dance?
Here it is, the second weekend after a Georgia Tech home game, and no tea dance is scheduled at any fraternity house. But perhaps you of the college set or of the young marrieds don't know about tea dances.

For years the "in" place after a Tech game was the tea dance at the Chi Phi fraternity house. It was somewhat of a tradition among the Chi Phi chapters at many Southern colleges. Dancing was from 5:00 to 7:00 P.M. Many of the stars of the football game attended and naturally were the lions of the hour. And going to a Chi Phi tea dance was a status symbol for a girl.

The Chi Phis were recognized as the pioneers of the tea dance custom, but later on, other fraternities got in on the act. The tea-dance craze spread city-wide, in a manner of speaking, and the Biltmore Hotel [now closed] held similar functions every Saturday afternoon, football season or not. These affairs, during the football season, were very popular, especially for the out-of-town visitors.

All these happenings were in the late twenties and in the thirties and forties. No one can give a reasonable answer as to

why these dances faded on the social calendar. The popularity just wore out.

Attempts have been made to revive the tea-dance custom, but to date, the idea has not scored among the social set.

Several do come to mind which were fun, however.

Margaret Duval, who was a member of the 1969-1970 Atlanta Debutante Club, made her bow at a tea dance at the Swan Coach House given by her parents, Mr. and Mrs. Fred Duval. It was a great party, and was something new to the debutante set.

Last year four girls who were presented by the Phoenix Society made their bow at a tea dance at the Sheraton-Biltmore Hotel, with their parents as hosts.

They were Sally Sullivant, daughter of Mr. and Mrs. John N. Sullivant, Jr.; Macy Fisher, daughter of Mr. and Mrs. James Fisher; Kathleen Hounsom, daughter of Mr. and Mrs.

John Hounsom; and Anne Collins, daughter of Mr. and Mrs. Joe Collins.

It was one of the largest parties of the season and took place in the hotel ballroom. But the tea-dance idea was once again a "first" for the girls and their dates.

Before the Phoenix Society moved its June presentation party from the Capital City Country Club to the Galleria of the Memorial Arts Center, a tea dance honored the incoming debutantes. When the location was switched, so was the event; now it is a supper dance.

For many years members of the Nine O'Clocks held a tea dance at the Piedmont Driving Club after the annual meeting. No more, though. Members of this oldest men's social group in the city hold their meeting and then do some drinking at a post-meeting stag cocktail party. Wives and girl friends are sitting at their homes twiddling their thumbs, and often having a drink themselves.

In the midsummer one of the largest parties of the season was a tea dance at the Driving Club given by a group of Atlantans to honor some newcomers to the city. It was the real thing, too, for all the guests were of the tea-dance generation.

On the whole, though, the tea dance is really a thing of the past. People would rather go to a cocktail party in the afternoon and stand on one foot, then the other, while sipping their favorite drink. They would rather dance at an evening party.

And for the record, a tea dance in its original form was a dance at which afternoon tea was served.

Fourth of July
Now Means BYOL

July 3, 1974

L AND SAKES! Even the political parties have changed. The women are wearing long summertime cottons and the men are wearing their sports jackets.

The cocktail party is the "in" thing.

With tomorrow being the Fourth of July, the thoughts of many are exploding like firecrackers down Memory Lane.

What has happened to the old-time Fourth of July barbecues which candidates used to give? They were usually the kickoff for the campaign. Maybe you recall them. The folks, as well as the flies, from the surrounding counties gathered at the focal site for the barbecue. Sometimes it was under a big tent, but more often under that hot Georgia sunshine. But, either place, they would eat spicy barbecue, hot Brunswick stew (always prepared right on the spot), potato salad and pickles. A band played somewhere, and small children who had come along for the food were running around waving flags and screaming.

After the eating orgy, the candidate would mount a flag-draped platform to make a fiery, arm-waving speech, saying he would lead them to the promised land with a bagful of benefits.

So far this year the political barbecue has become a cocktail party. Sometimes the candidate is host, sometimes he (or she) is the guest of honor.

The parties are being given in the best social style. Several have been at poolside, some at a penthouse. One last week was a large al fresco event.

The other night there was a big cocktail party in the West Paces Ferry Road section. Invitations were issued on folded cards, the cover being a pen and ink sketch of the State Capitol. The party was complete with caterer. No speeches, no pamphlets and no campaign buttons as favors. But the guests got the word—VOTE. The usual cocktail party for a candidate is just like any other party for a VIP. However, at the candidate's party, the host, with studied strategy, leads a guest over to the honoree and says, "You know Alexander the Great, he has been looking forward to meeting you. I'll just leave you two here to chat a while." He gets your name, address, zip code and phone number before you know it.

At many of these parties a guest is given a name tag like those at a convention. It says, "Hello, my name is. . . ." At one party, a woman guest wore her name tag, which she had signed, and it read, "Hello, I am a Brownie Scout Troop Leader." The candidate won't forget her!

There is hope for the voters who have been missing that good old Georgia sunshine at the open-air eating marathons. There is going to be a big gathering for all the gubernatorial candidates in Gainesville on the Fourth. But it won't be the same. It's a BYOL party.

If you think that it means the usual thing (bring your own liquor), you are wrong. It means, "bring your own lunch!"

Little Things
Mean A Lot

SMALL KINDNESSES, small courtesies, and small considerations habitually practiced in our social dealings give a greater charm to the character than the display of great talents and accomplishments.

There are few things more important than putting our character into the little habits and deeds of the day.

The famed Henry Clay once remarked that, "the courtesies of a small and trivial character are the ones which strike deepest to the grateful and appreciating heart."

A churlish, careless hello over the telephone or on the street is an enemy to the finest responses of which men are capable.

Both business and social contacts call for studied grace and goodness of character, if they are to be productive of success and happiness.

The Trouble Basket

THIS FEATURE WAS published during the early 1940s as a "clearing house for problems of the heart and mind."

Dear Miss Gwin:

I have read all the advice and all the articles in the books and papers and magazines on how to attract a man. I have used the advice, but I am still manless. I am coming to you as a last resort. Why don't the rules work? What must I do?

Helpless

Dear Helpless:

Perhaps if you would *stop* trying to act according to rules, things would be better and you could get the man of your dreams. If I were you, I would take all the books and magazines and throw them away. Then I would use some good, common sense and a few feminine wiles. After all, men are not some strange race of people that you have to treat according to rules. They are people just like you and I, and there are as many types as there are flowers in a garden. Each has to be cultivated in a different way. You just have to analyze the man you want and treat him accordingly. Forget the rules! A rule for one may not work for another, so there you are. Nine out of ten men are very easy to get along with, so don't be too hopeless.

Dear Miss Gwin:

Eight years ago John and I became engaged. We still love each other and hope to marry some day, but it seems as if everything has gone against us. John lost his job, and the one he has now does not pay very well. He has obligations to his family which must be met. I work and have to support my mother as well as myself. If we marry, it will mean added responsibilities, but the years are going by, and John and I are not getting any younger. What do you think we should do—take a chance at life, regardless of our obligations, or wait with the hope that things will be better? This life is not very happy, and neither John nor I have very much hope for the future, as the situation now stands. What is your advice?

Mabel and John

Dear Mabel and John:

My advice to you is to marry now. I can understand your responsibilities, and the feelings you both have in trying to meet them and your self-imposed obligations to your families. However, I think you both have your own lives to lead, and the sooner you begin the better it will be. As long as you remain single, there will be these same obligations, and perhaps many more. I believe that, married, you two could find a few years' happiness, at least. Too many men and women have wasted their entire lives, believing that family responsibilities were of first consideration. I think, but not from a selfish standpoint, that you should think of yourselves now and marry. Things will adjust themselves and will be all right.

Dear Miss Gwin:

I am going away to camp in a few days, and I would like to write to a boy I know while I am there. Will you tell me how long after I leave home would be the proper time to write? Must I ask him to answer the letter?

Camper

Dear Camper:

I think a week after you arrive at camp would be soon enough to write him. Tell him the news about camp and how you like it, and finish by asking him to write and tell you all the news.

Dear Miss Gwin:

This is a situation which has me stumped. My wife and I have never been able to agree on vacations, so we always take separate ones; she goes her way and I go mine. This year she is going to the East and I have decided to go on a cruise. Everything is ready for the trip and I have been looking forward to going, but now here come the fireworks. A good friend of my wife has decided to go on the same trip, and I am on the spot because my wife thinks that it was prearranged. Of course, it was not, and I had no idea that she was going, but since she is, my wife has been raising Cain for several weeks. To make matters worse, this woman is an attractive widow, and I know there will be some talk, because naturally we will be thrown together while on the trip. What do you think I had better do—cancel my trip or go on, knowing what the gossip might be? My wife tells me that, if I loved her, I would not go. Hurry up and answer, so I can either catch the boat or cancel the trip.

J. L. C.

Dear J. L. C.:

I think you would be very foolish to miss such a grand trip because this attractive widow is going to be on board. Go on and enjoy yourself, and don't pay any attention to what the gossip will be, nor to what your wife says. I should think that your wife would be glad to know someone she knows is going along, rather than to think you may run into some strange women, whose prey are married men "on leave." My advice to you on this trip will be to always see to it that you and the attractive widow are "among those present" at all the ship parties and not all alone on the deck in the moonlight. If you must see the ocean at night, I think you had better see it with some of your new-found cruise companions.

Dear Miss Gwin:

I would like your advice on the subject of my second marriage. I am a divorcée, and since I left my husband I have been living in a small town. Because I am a divorcée, the people don't think so much of me. Of course, I do not care much what they think, for they are all narrow-minded, anyway, but I would like to have the correct kind of wedding for my second attempt. They will talk, whatever I do, but for my own satisfaction I want to have everything just so. I live with an aunt and uncle, and they have told me they will give me any type of wedding I want. Please give me some advice on the subject.

Divorcée

Dear Divorcée:

Well, in the first place, I suppose the townspeople consider you a stain on the family escutcheon, and are old-fashioned in the belief that divorcées should take their place in the closet reserved for sad and shady subjects. I don't blame you for not caring what they say, for there are times when a divorce is the only and the happiest solution.

As for the wedding, a divorcée, or the woman who marries for the second time, should not think of wearing white. She usually wears street clothes, or a long afternoon dress, with a hat. If she so desires, she may have one attendant, but hardly more. A large wedding is definitely out; only the families and the very close friends are invited, and the reception is correspondingly small. I think if I were you, I would plan a small wedding at the home of the uncle and aunt, and make it as small and dignified as possible. Of course, you know that when a divorcée remarries, she takes off her first wedding ring and seldom wears her first engagement ring.

Dear Miss Gwin:

Please give me a few pointers on how to be popular. I would rather be popular than anything else I know of, and I need some help in a hurry.

Wallflower

Dear Wallflower:

The first thing to do would be to change your name from "Wallflower" to "Belle of the Ball." If you think you are a wallflower, then you will be one. Self-consciousness seems to be the stuff of which all wallflowers are made, so the thing for you to do is to snap out of that idea.

People who have friends are popular; so the thing for you to do is to gain friends, and gain as many as you can. It takes years of hard work to make and keep friends, and the main point is to sell yourself to the other fellow. Don't be backward and standoffish. Don't expect the other fellow to do all the advancing and the running. You have got to do your part. Friendship is a give-and-take proposition. If there is something about a person you like, why not cultivate the trait yourself and see how well it works on your acquaintances? Being popular is going out and winning friends by being enthusiastic and showing determination that they will be your friends for keeps. Sit down and make a list of things which you would like for people to do to and for you. Use that list on other people, and you will see that what you sow, you will reap. Don't have ego—don't think that everything you do, you say, or you think is perfect. Be generous, be considerate, and be sympathetic of other people and of their feelings. To sum it all up, it amounts to the old saying of, "do unto others as you would have others do unto you." A good definition of a friend is this: A person who knows us and still likes us.

Dear Miss Gwin:

I am a newcomer to Atlanta, and I went to a dance recently and was introduced to an attractive girl. I would like very much to have a date with her, but I am afraid that she will not remember me. What must I do?

Jim W.

Dear Jim W.:

Call the girl and tell her your name, and, if it doesn't register, tell her the name of the boy who introduced you. Ask her for a date, and if she gives you one, the rest is left to you—if you know what I mean.

Dear Miss Gwin:

A boy has asked me to wear his fraternity pin. I have never had one before, and I wonder if it means that I will be engaged to him? It is a pretty pin, and I would like to wear it.

High School Girl

Dear High School Girl:

By wearing the boy's pin, you identify him as your favorite beau, but it is not a definite sign you are engaged to him, so I would not consider it that way.

I do hope you are not going to take the pin just because it is pretty. I think you had better be a bit more fair to the boy than that and take the pin because you like him and consider him your favorite. If you like him, and he asked you to wear his pin, you would take it if it were pretty or not, wouldn't you? And, another thing—don't collect too many pins at the same time, either.

Dear Miss Gwin:

Do you think long engagements are advisable? The boy I am in love with has at least seven more years of study before he will become a doctor, and he wants me to wait for him. I love him, but I don't think it is fair for him to ask me to give up all my friends and not go out any more. He does not live here, and wherever he is I am sure that he will not be as isolated as I would be. What do you think?

Betty

Dear Betty:

I think that seven years is a rather long time for you to sit at home and wait for your Dream Prince to return. It is very seldom that long engagements have a happy ending. People change, and they often develop different habits and viewpoints. Both of you might have lost the glamour which attracted you in the beginning. Just lay your cards on the table. Tell your young man to go on with his studies, that you will go your way and will continue to love him, but will not sit on the anxious bench waiting for him. Tell him that if, after seven years, he is ready to talk business, he should come around. If you both feel then as you do now, the separation will have served as a test of your love.

Dear Miss Gwin:

I am not interested in girls, but the few I know seem to think that I am. I don't want to be rude, but I am just not interested in going to parties, having dates and running around. What would you suggest I do, when the girls keep calling me up and inviting me places?

Bachelor

Dear Bachelor:

If I were you, I wouldn't be worried about the girls calling. From your attitude, I feel sure that the girls who seem to be giving you the rush will soon discover your feelings on the subject and will not bore you with their invitations. Remember that there always have to be extra men at a party, so I wouldn't take the invitations too seriously. When the girls refuse *your* dates—and I am sure you do have them—you soon take the hint and fade out of the picture, don't you?

Dear Miss Gwin:

I am sixteen years old and have been wearing a boy's fraternity pin for several months. I like this boy very much, but there is someone else I like, too. This last boy has asked me to wear his pin, but he doesn't know I have one that belongs to someone else. What would you do? Tell him I have a pin, or take his and have them both?

Joyce

Dear Joyce:

Why not take fraternity pin No. 2? You must never let your right hand know what your left hand is doing, you know, and, after all, it is not a bad idea to have two admirers on the string. I feel sure that you can be true to both the boys, but there is a limit to everything, even fraternity pins, and there is no use in being a collector and establishing a reputation of being fickle. When you become a little older, you will know how to handle a lot of men, making each think he is the one and only.

Dear Miss Gwin:

I am going to be married soon, and I would like to know a point of etiquette. The presents are arriving daily, and I would like to know about thank-you notes. When should they be written?

Bride-To-Be

Dear Bride-To-Be:

Write the notes the day you receive the gift.

Good Nature Is
Requisite of Charm

GOOD NATURE in all circumstances is one of the greatest single assets in the world. The famous Lady Mendel once said that in her girlhood, her mother advised her to be "pretty if you can, witty if you must, but be agreeable if it kills you."

The social woman keeps in touch with everyone she knows, and the pushy woman pursues those whose friendship will benefit her. One woman is motivated by a love of people, the other by a love of position. Those who climb the slippery social ladder by main force usually pay too much for what they gain and often lose it in the end.

Too many people start out on their chosen careers without ever giving a thought to the most valuable tool they can use—personal magnetism. They burn the midnight oil to gather as much technical knowledge as they can, yet they leave it to Lady Luck to give them what she will of the charm they could acquire on their own.

Yolande's Atlanta

The First Hundred Years

Atlanta's Social Hunger
Had to Be Satisfied

July 26, 1964

THE SOCIAL METEOR has been whirling through the skies over Atlanta for one hundred years. Its brilliance has been dimmed several times by war clouds, but even these have not slowed its journey into the uncharted social space.

The start was slow. After the War Between the States, Atlantans were more interested in repairing the battle damages than in partying. Yet, the social hunger had to be satisfied.

During the Christmas season of 1867, a group of young men, back in their civvies after wearing Confederate gray, hired a carriage and went calling on young Atlanta belles. Calling hours began about noon, and sometimes the young men made as many as twenty calls during the day. Thus, this social custom began in Atlanta.

The warm sunshine during the summer of 1868 lured society into the open for carefree merriment. The Regatta at Peachtree Creek was one of the social highlights of June. Atlantans piled into bandwagons drawn by six horses to travel from Howell's store in midtown Atlanta out Peachtree to Peachtree Creek. Families sat on the grass and ate picnic lunches. Many entered swimming meets.

One of the most popular pastimes of society was visiting Walton Spring and the Mineral Spring, which hit an all-time high in popularity in 1868. Located at the latter, Spring Hill Cottage was commodious and well-planned for those who enjoyed dining and dancing. There were two saloons—one each for the ladies and gentlemen—and on the second story of the building was a fine, level "plaza" for dancing.

During the early 1870s, a group of prominent young men banded together in a secret order they called the Mystic Brotherhood. In 1873 they staged a gay carnival, with a parade led by King Rex. The next year society gathered at De Give's Opera House for a masked ball after the parade.

As the years slipped by, the social spotlight moved to famous Peachtree Street. The street became the center for gracious living, as did its connecting streets and avenues. During the years from 1875 to 1880, Atlanta society gathered for garden parties and evening parties. The latter affairs featured bridge and euchre parties, always held on the wide porches of Atlanta homes. One of the largest social events of 1875 was the Grand Fete at Oglethorpe Park, which gathered several hundred Atlantans. It was an all-day affair with spirited sporting events such as football, foot races, and such popular English games as quoits and cricket.

The small-fry went to Glenn and Wright's new hall for roller skating parties. Birthday parties given there were the rage for years. Would-be skaters were given the advice, "Never try to skate in two directions at once."

A social note of the period, causing much chatter, was the news that Mrs. Stonewall Jackson had declined an offer of marriage.

In 1878, two institutions were born which would be important links in Atlanta's social chain. Aristocratic in its formation was Washington Seminary, which was founded by Anita and Lola Washington, nieces of Lawrence Washington, who was a half brother of George Washington. Its last site was where the Riviera Motel now stands. It merged with the Westminster Schools in 1953.

The Bell House was also an important social mark in the city from 1878 until its doors closed in 1950. Widowed at twenty-four, with two children, Mrs. Emma Bell opened a home for bachelors and widowers. As the years passed, her home became a status address for young men of the city, so there was always a long waiting list. Mrs. Bell had strict rules for her "boys," although she was not averse to parties, and many an Atlanta belle cherished an invitation to attend an open house given at the Bell House. Among Mrs. Bell's rules: No drinking in the house, no smoking in the dining rooms, and all boarders had to wear their coats while sitting on the verandas and while dining, hot weather notwithstanding.

In 1883 another step was placed on Atlanta's social walkway. In March of that year thirty-one young men formed the Nine O'Clock German Club. It was strictly a social group, and the balls began promptly at 9:00 P.M. and ended at 12:00 P.M. All were held at the Kimball House, the city's most fashionable gathering place. However, with the passing of years, the balls were transferred to the Piedmont Driving Club, where they are still held. During World War I, the name "German" was dropped from the title and it became known, as it still is today, as the Nine O'Clocks. It is the oldest active social organization in the city.

Another social organization which was formed "to promote the pleasure, kind feeling and general culture of its members" was the Capital City Club, chartered in May of 1883 by eighty-two social and business leaders in the bustling little city of Atlanta. Over the years the club has been the gathering place of local and visiting bigwigs. The first clubhouse was on the southeast corner of Walton and Fairlie streets. In 1884, the club moved to its second location, now the site of Davison's. The present building at Peachtree and Harris streets was dedicated in 1911. The country club at Brookhaven was bought in 1913.

The Piedmont Driving Club, long a center of social activity, was organized in 1887, but at the time was called the Gentlemen's Driving Club. Its specific object was the association of club members for the purpose of driving fine horses. During the fall of 1887, in anticipation of the great Exposition, the club purchased the entire grounds of what is now Piedmont Park. Subsequently, all the club's land was sold to the Piedmont Exposition Company, which had successfully operated the Exposition of 1887. But the Gentlemen's Driving Club continued in existence and in 1895 the Piedmont Driving Club charter was obtained. In 1897 the Piedmont Exposition Company conveyed to the Piedmont Driving Club the grounds where the club now stands, on Piedmont Avenue facing the Fifteenth Street intersection. The Driving Club has been the center of brilliant social events, dances, debut parties, wedding receptions, etc., over the years. Social clubs have been formed within its walls, and for years it has been the setting for the official presentation of Atlanta debutantes.

As did similar groups in other cities in the nation, Atlanta society began the last ten years of the nineteenth century in a mood of high living and expanding social life.

Cotillions were held in private homes, in clubs and at the Kimball House. Summertime parties were still garden fetes, but the vogue to charter a streetcar for the nine-mile ride around the city soon found belles and beaux choosing this form of entertainment. "Open houses" on Christmas and New Year's Day were still social events of the fading year, and newspapers published lists of the hostesses who would be "at home" to their friends.

Society turned out in full force for the opening of Laurent

De Give's new opera house—later to become Loew's Grand Theater—in 1893. Box parties were preceded by dinner parties at private homes and clubs. The event was a social highlight of the year.

As dances continued to be popular, the young people danced the two-step and the Boston Dip. The girl who could dip the lowest was the belle of the ball.

In 1898 sixty-five young businessmen desiring a place to gather for physical exercise decided to form the Atlanta Athletic Club. The first building was on Edgewood Avenue, and later the clubhouse was on Auburn Avenue. The club became so popular that a country club at East Lake was formed in 1908. Family parties gathered there for boating, swimming, barbecues and outdoor events, and the place was termed by society writers of the day as "just what Atlanta needed." In 1926, the town club was moved into its present location on Carnegie Way. It has been a social center for years, and the roof garden for dining and dancing has been one of the favorite spots for partying. In 1958 the third link in the club chain was formed—the Yacht Club at Lake Lanier.

The activities of the Butterfly Club during the early years of the new century were of a social nature. Members were social leaders of the city's distaff side, who met for quilting parties, spend-the-day parties, and Virginia Reels.

The early years of the twentieth century also saw the Jewish community organize the Standard Club. Formed in 1905, the club had its first building on Washington Street, and then, as the city grew, club members built a place on Ponce de Leon Avenue. After two decades there, the club moved to its present location in northeast Atlanta on Standard Drive in the Roxboro Road area.

Young ladies of society "finished" at Woodberry Hall, formed in 1908 by Rosa Woodberry, the first woman student at the University of Georgia. It is no longer in existence as a school, but its last building is still on Peachtree Circle.

The North Avenue Presbyterian Church opened its school in September of 1909 in the church building. Locations on North and Ponce de Leon avenues served until 1951, when the North Avenue Presbyterian School moved to a tract of land bought from Fritz Orr and became the Westminster Schools.

A social milestone for the city was the formation of Atlanta's first Debutante Club in 1911. The club is still in existence, with the activities of its members adding sparkle to the social scene. The girls bowing that year were officially presented at the Halloween Ball at the Piedmont Driving Club. The affair inaugurated the formal winter social season in the city, a tradition which is still followed.

The Druid Hills Golf Club, organized in 1912, has long been one of the social gathering places and golf sites for Atlanta. When the club opened, the *Atlanta Journal* reported that, "The Ponce de Leon Avenue car, which now stops at the Lullwater Bridge, will at once be extended out one-half mile so as to afford easy access to the club house."

For years society gathered for al fresco parties on the wide terraces of the Druid Hills club. Fires and remodeling have dotted its history, but again in the 1960s members and their guests were gathering for outdoor dining and dancing around the pool.

The golf course in Ansley Park was laid out in 1910 and completed in 1912. In 1913 a group of men who played the course regularly objected to paying the fifty-cent green fee. So, in 1915, they formed the Ansley Park Golf Club and obtained a charter. The name was changed to the Ansley Golf Club in 1951. The clubhouse has been enlarged several times, and the club's annals are filled with entries of many gay social events.

In 1914, a group of young Jewish citizens formed the Osceola Club. Later, to enlarge the membership, the group formed the Progressive Club and built a big clubhouse on Pryor Street. In 1941, the club moved and built the massive building on Techwood Drive, which was doubled in size in 1949 and added to again in 1964. Today it is the home of Ted Turner's television empire.

Despite a streetcar strike in October of 1916, the girls who had been debutantes in the clubs of 1914, 1915 and 1916, met and organized the Atlanta Junior League. When the group was less than a month old, it sponsored the Butterfly Ball, which was one of the highlights of the fall season. In 1920 its first Follies was presented. Nineteen years later, at the city auditorium, the League gave its biggest production, the *Gone With the Wind* Ball, to celebrate the world premiere of the movie version of the famed novel by Atlanta's Margaret Mitchell.

During the years of World War I, social affairs continued, but took on a decidedly military flavor. There were tea dances at the Piedmont Driving Club, honoring officers stationed at Fort McPherson and Camp Gordon, and society backed Red Cross charity balls one hundred percent.

The men in uniform were also entertained by Governor and Mrs. Hugh Dorsey, who lived in the executive mansion on the present site of the Henry Grady Hotel.

The social spotlight hovered over the mansion almost daily, for in addition to the visits of official and military figures, there was the usual activity of political life. The Dorseys kept in step with other social goings-on in the city, too. The governor's niece, Mary Faith Yow of Lavonia, spent the winter at the mansion the year she made her debut in Atlanta society and the big house rang with merriment. Although debut parties were given there during the season, the mansion's debutante made her formal bow at a dance given by the Dorseys at the nearby Capital City Club. Among the guests who gathered to honor the debutante, who became Mrs. A. G. Adams of Coral Gables, Florida, was General John J. Pershing.

After World War I, a group of friends began gathering for social affairs in private homes. When the number amounted to fifty, it was decided to form the Mayfair Club. During the twenties, meetings in the form of dances and dinner parties were held at the Atlanta Biltmore Hotel. As the club grew in number, members decided to build a clubhouse and bought property on Spring Street, near the intersection of Peachtree. The building was erected in 1939, and was the center of many social events during the years. Although the building was destroyed by fire in December of 1963, the Mayfair Club, as a social group, is still in existence.

Atlantans entered the Roarin' Twenties in the same manner as the rest of the nation—they danced the Charleston. They also went to tea dances at the Georgia Tech fraternity houses after football games. Atlanta's belles met their dates downtown at Nunnally's ice cream parlor.

The college set danced—as they had for years—at Sedgalos on Pine Street between the Peachtrees. In the early years of the twenties, Garber Hall, named for bandleader Jan Garber who played there, was the gathering place for the college set on Friday and Saturday nights. The hall, on the southwest corner of Peachtree Street and North Avenue, was the site of scrip dances held under the sponsorship of Georgia Tech and Emory campus leaders. Atlanta mothers, sometimes as many as twenty, lined one side of the dance hall as chaperones.

Horseback riding has always been among the hobbies enjoyed by Atlantans. Many social events marked the activities of the Saddle and Sirloin Club, which was formed in the early twenties. Some twenty years later, the Shakerag

Hounds was formed, a hunting group whose hunt balls and breakfast parties enliven the social calendar.

Also in the twenties, tea dances became more and more popular. The Atlanta Biltmore Hotel inaugurated a weekly series, and many private clubs began the custom. Dining and dancing on the roof gardens of the Capital City Club and the Atlanta Athletic Club attracted society during the hot summer months. Mah-jongg replaced bridge as the afternoon party pastime, and Atlantans gathered at homes to play and have tea parties.

During the thirties, keeping pace with the rest of the world, Atlanta society began to gather instead for the cocktail hour. Tea dances lost their popularity, but partying continued.

War was to come again to cast its shadow over the merriment which Atlanta so loved.

After December 7, 1941, the social pace slowed down. Men left the city for military service. The debutantes of 1942-1943 canceled many large parties due to the war. Patio parties became "the thing" to have. Porch parties—such as bridge and supper affairs—were no longer on the social list. Porches were going out of style.

Building style was to carve another niche in Atlanta's social life. Churches were either enlarging or adding on "great halls" or recreation rooms. Wedding receptions in the brides' homes soon lost popularity. It seemed easier, and certainly cheaper, to have the wedding reception at the church.

The fashion was an immediate success. In the years that have followed, church receptions have become more and more fashionable.

During the forties, while most of the hometown men were away, men from other cities were doing military duty in

Atlanta. Every Tuesday evening officers gathered at the Georgian Terrace Hotel to dance with the local belles who, after exclusive selection, had become members of the Girls Battalion. Many a wartime marriage was the result of these dances.

After the war, members of the Battalion decided not to disband, but to continue as a group and have dances. The result was the formation of the Assemblies, which still hold one large ball each year and invite the city's most popular young girls to become members.

The Peachtree Golf Club is an important as well as historical link in Atlanta's social chain. The white-columned house is over one hundred years old. In 1903 it was bought by the late W. T. Ashford to become the center of the wide area known as Ashford Park Nurseries. Mrs. Ashford's daughter, Mrs. Cobb Caldwell, sold it in 1945 to the group of men who were to form the Peachtree Golf Club in 1947. Atlanta's Bobby Jones was the guiding spirit in the formation of the club, as well as in the laying out of the golf course in 1948. Today the club has its full membership of 225. The big house and grounds form the setting for many of the city's most distinguished parties.

Social groups began to spring up around the city after World War II. One was the Peachtree Racket Club. In November of 1946, two of the group which subsequently founded the club were offered a place to hold a New Year's Eve party if they could organize a club. The place was the big, red barn on the property of Sharpe Wall on Northside Drive. It was not until five days before New Year's Eve that the planners were definite about their party. With couples invited, the party was a big success. And the name? The founding fathers of the club decided that, since the object of the club was to get together and raise a racket, the name "Racket" was both appropriate and descriptive. The prefix,

Peachtree, so universally expressive of Atlanta, was added for obvious reasons. The official title of all club events is "racket," not "party." There are two functions a year, one in the spring and the other on New Year's Eve. Membership includes one hundred prominent couples among Atlanta's social ranks.

In addition to social clubs, physical expressions of the city's social growth began to appear. The Cherokee Town and Country Club was formed and its charter granted in 1956. The clubhouse on West Paces Ferry Road is the former John W. Grant home, one of the landmarks of the north side.

The fifties were filled with news of the formation of new clubs in the city. The University Yacht Club at Lake Lanier was organized in 1951. As the name implies, all members own boats. The name, "University," reflects the fact that club members are graduates of leading colleges and universities.

The social spotlight also shines on another lake where Atlantans party. A group of enthusiastic young men formed the Allatoona Yacht Club in 1952. The colonial-style clubhouse was completed and formally opened in 1956.

The Atlanta Yacht Club—this is a sailing club—was organized in 1950. A clubhouse overlooks Lake Allatoona, and the adjacent area is dotted with many homes belonging to Atlantans. There are year-round activities, as well as many private events.

Another social club organized in the fifties was Lakeside Country Club, whose members have been culled from leaders in the East Point, College Park, and Cascade Heights areas. The big clubhouse is modern in style and is located on Old Fairburn Road. The annual president's ball is one of the social highlights among the membership.

The Benedicts was founded in 1958. Members who had been in high school and college together banded together to further strengthen their ties of friendship. There are one hundred and twenty members, most of whom are married, hence the name Benedicts. They give two parties a year, a dinner dance on New Year's Eve and a springtime fancy-dress ball.

Another group of young men, just out of high school and some in their first year of college, formed the Gentry Club in the late fifties. Strictly social in nature, the club gives parties at specified times of the year.

In 1959 a group of men formed the Castle View Town and Country Club. Initial plans called for a club in Buckhead on Pharr Road, facilities downtown, and a country club in Gwinnett County. Presently, club members are in the process of building onto and remodeling the Pharr Road building to complement the closing of the downtown branch. The golf club remains, with an eighteen-hole course.

The sixties will go down in social history as the period when two new debutante groups were formed to complement the long-established Atlanta Debutante Club formed in 1911.

The Phoenix Society, composed of a group of Atlanta businessmen, organized in May of 1964. The members will present to society each year a selected group of Atlanta girls. The society is based on a tradition like the St. Cecelia Society of Charleston, the Bachelors' Cotillion of Baltimore, and the Veiled Prophets of St. Louis.

Close on the heels of the Phoenix Society came the Cherokee Debutantes. These girls are daughters of members of the Cherokee Town and Country Club. This organization, like the Phoenix Society, is another milestone along the Atlanta's social path, for it marks the first time a debutante group has been formed within a social club.

The German Club, formed in 1962, is an outgrowth of a meeting of longtime friends who wanted to get together for a

New Year's party. When the club was formed, a majority of its members were young married couples, and it sponsored three parties a year, a New Year's Eve fancy dress ball, a Derby Day party and a summer function.

Now, in the last half of the twentieth century, the social meteor is still whirling, but its pace is faster, faster, faster.

Yolande's Atlanta

Reminiscences

Broken Bones, Ozark Pudding, and Famous Dogs

THIS DIALOGUE between Yolande Gwin and Jack
Spalding took place as a program at the Atlanta
Historical Society on March 8, 1981.

JACK: I think she's on a first-name basis with everybody here
but, in case there's a stranger in the crowd, I'll hit some of the
high spots. First of all, she's of mixed ancestry. She's half
Mobile, half Boston. That makes her an all-American girl.
She has a great collection of flags to prove it. Maybe we'll get
into that later. She's been called the last of the great society
editors by our esteemed colleague, Hugh Richardson, Jr., of
the *Bowman News.* He is entirely correct. She is one of a long
line of great ones—Polly Peachtree, Sally Forth, Peachtree
Parade, Cherokee Charlie. American newspaper publishers
decided a few years ago that what we needed to read about was
social problems rather than fun and frolic. Yolande has
resisted that, God bless her.

She is also a great reporter. Most people identify her with
the society page, but she has gone 'way beyond that during
our time. I remember when Mr. Roosevelt came to
Barnesville, in '38 I think, to dedicate the first REA project

Yolande's desk was the depository for many gifts

in Georgia. He ended up trying to purge Senator Walter George. It was a big story; the press went wild. Senator George got up and accepted the challenge. It was electrifying news all over the country. Senator George had led the fight against Roosevelt's proposal to pack the Supreme Court. Yolande was on the platform. She had the most interesting story the next day. Mr. Roosevelt had forgotten to pull the switch to start the electrical juice flowing! She was the only reporter who saw that. She's a real trooper. You know these days when it rains and it freezes and the trees fall down and the wires fall down and the roads get slick, strong men stay home and don't go to work. Yolande gets there somehow. I don't know how; maybe she will tell us. Yolande is all that and a lot more. I like to think of her as Atlanta's best girl.

YOLANDE: Oh, Jack! That's the cutest thing.

JACK: Yolande has covered every sort of story imaginable. She graduated from Washington Seminary. She made her debut. She signed up for Sweet Briar, but she was offered a job on *The Atlanta Georgian*. She was born with printer's ink in her blood. One of her Mobile ancestors was a columnist on the *Mobile Register*. . . .Yolande will do almost anything to get to a good party. Once she was invited to a party in Americus, broke her ankle, but she wouldn't admit it was broken and went on, anyhow. She worked for a week, I think, on it.

YOLANDE: Yes, and then everybody in the office said, "You've got to go have your leg fixed," but I wanted to go to the party. I went down to the party. It was in Americus. There were five ladies who gave the party. It was a farewell party for Rosalynn Carter before she went up to Washington. They sent out engraved invitations, and my only objection to the engraved invitation is that they invited Mrs. Yolande Gwin, so I managed to spill a Coca-Cola on the *Mrs.* So, if anybody sees it, they'll think just, "That's Yolande Gwin." So, anyway, we went down there, and we were given orders when we arrived. It was a beautiful home, and I have forgotten whose home it was[1]—that's terrible, but I can't help it. It was a beautiful Victorian home in Americus, and there was a lady standing out in front and, when we walked up to the door, she said, "I'm just letting in twenty people at a time," and so the line was way down the street, you know. "I'm only letting in twenty people at a time because we don't want so many people in the house." Well, we stood there and waited, and finally we got in, and there was a woman at the

---

[1]Home of Wayne and Mary Dean

door inside, and she said, "Now speak to Mrs. Carter and then go on into the living room." So we all said, "Hello," and they pushed us away; we couldn't say anything else—hello, goodbye—and then we got to the door to go into the living room and there was another lady. And she said, "Now, don't anybody take off your coat and put it on the chairs or on the sofas. Just keep them on or carry them." Well, I was about to burn up. We finally got inside, and I wandered around—oh, incidentally, Mrs. Sam Meyer drove me down there because her sister was one of the hostesses, and she had left me and said she was going on in. I was standing there in the living room, just looking around trying to envision what I was going to write about, casing the joint, in other words, when somebody came in and said, "Oh, Yolande, what am I going to do? I'm about to burn up." And I turned around and it was the First Lady of Alabama, Cornelia Wallace; she had on a full-length white ermine coat. She said it was cold when they flew over from Montgomery. I said, "Well, after all, you *are* the First Lady of Alabama and you've got rights; do what you want to." And she said, "Oh, I'll just sweat it out." Last time I saw her she was fanning herself with the sleeve of the coat, which was still on.

So I went on into the dining room, and there stood another lady. And she said, "Now, lady, have some refreshments, whatever you want, and then please go out the back door of the dining room into the hallway and out into the yard." And I thought to myself, "That's not a very nice way to be saying, 'Get out the back way.'" I thought, "I've got to get a story on Rosalynn Carter." I happened that day to be wearing a necklace that one of my dear friends, Clara Belle King, had given me for my birthday, and it had one of those—remember those old Coca-Cola openers that you used to have on the wall?—well, I have a necklace with that hanging on it.

Anyway, one time working at the Coach House I had it on, and Rosalynn was over there buying some things for the children for Christmas, and she said, "Oh, did you get this here? This is the cutest thing I ever saw." And I told her who gave it to me.

Anyway, I thought as I started to the back door, "I'm not going out this back door—I don't have enough for my story. Nothing to it except Cornelia Wallace burning up." So I looked around a little bit and there was a little hallway that went back to the entrance hall and I could see Rosalynn right up there. I thought, "Well, I'm going to pretend I'm looking at the house." So I edged a little bit at a time, and went on closer and closer, and I finally got in the back of the hall. And there stood a great big man with his arms folded and he said, "Lady, you can't come any farther." And I said, "I was just looking at all the pretty things in your house." And he said, "You mustn't get any closer." And the horrible part about it was, I had my walking stick with me, too, because my ankle hurt so badly. He saw the walking stick and then he looked at his wrist. I thought to myself, "Ah hah! you're the Secret Service man!" He had one of those walkie-talkie radios, and I kept getting closer and closer, you know, and finally got up as close as I could, and he turned around again and said, "Lady, you can't come in here." And I said, "Oh, I'm so sorry, did I push you? I was just looking at all these pretty pictures in here." And about that time the front door closed, so Rosalynn could have a rest and kick off her shoes and catch her breath from the crowd, and she happened to look down the hall, and she said, "Hey, Yolande, where's the Coca-Cola necklace?" And I looked at the man and I said, "See, she knows me." He said, "All right, lady, I'm sorry, go on in and talk to her for a while." And I'll have you know, I went out the *front* door.

JACK: After that she went to see a doctor about her ankle.

YOLANDE: Then I spent two months at Piedmont. But I did get the story, and Rosalynn told me some nice things, and I wrote a long piece about it, and it worked out all right. So you see, if anybody in here is trying to be a reporter, you've got to climb in windows, and lie, and push Secret Service men around.

JACK: Not only that, you have to answer the telephone a hundred times a day. Not all your calls are pleasant. Not all your callers are sane. Or people come to see you, and they are not all pleasant, and about half of them are insane, wouldn't you think?

YOLANDE: Well, of course they are.

JACK: I remember a caller came to see me on the old *Constitution,* and came up to my desk. I was writing feature stories then, and he says, "I've got a story for you." I said, "What?" He opened this box and he said, "My wife had a tumor out and it's so big and elastic I just want you to see it and take a picture of it."

Yolande has had her share of that. I remember one letter she got—I see a lot of our old cohorts here, Sue Brown Sterne, Margaret Stovall, Dana McGee, Bunky Witham; they've all shared in these occasions. I remember a letter she got one morning from a lady down in south Georgia wanting her daughter's engagement announced, and she did the usual things, you know, what high school she graduated from, what college, grandparents and all that. And then to really give it a little punch she says, "Her grandfather was a lineman with Southern Bell and saw the last public hanging in Georgia."

YOLANDE: As Jack says, we get all kinds of crazy letters, and I've been saving them, and the *Journal* just recently dropped the method of using engagements, but I have all those letters. . . . You've never seen the equal of women whose daughters get married. They just go crazy, absolutely insane, and I will give you one illustration to show you what methods they go through.

I got home late one afternoon, in the winter, and it was dark, and I do carry a pistol all the time. I have a derringer and I have a .22 and I have a .45. . . . all over the house. Don't anybody break in—there are pistols hidden everywhere! I had just gotten in. I had on my coat, and had my derringer in my pocket, and I didn't have my little dog then—he would have let out a squeal if he heard anybody at the door.

Somebody knocked on the door, and I cracked it a little bit and I said, "Who is it?" And this woman was standing there and she didn't look like anybody I'd seen in Rich's or on the bus, and she said, "Miss Gwin, I have something for you," and she had a great big thing in her hand. I flicked the light on the outside so I could take a look at her, and I said, "That's so nice of you," and I put my hand in my pocket to be sure the derringer was there. "Won't you come in?"

She said, "Oh, I have come out because I know you girls that work on the paper hate to come home and have to cook, so I have cooked you a tuna casserole." And I said, "Well, that's so nice of you." She said, "Everybody says my tuna casserole is the best in the whole world. For one thing, I use hard-cooked eggs in mine, and I don't cut the eggs crosswise, I slice them longways." She told me all about how to make a tuna fish casserole. Anybody can do it if you have a can of tuna and a can of Campbell's soup; you know that. And I said, "I know it's wonderful. Suppose you let me take it and put it in one of my casserole dishes and wash your dish so you can take it home." "Oh, no, I wouldn't think of it, you keep the whole thing." And she told me a dozen times that her friends always called her to do the tuna fish casserole at the bridge party and at everything they had. And I said, "Well, I know I'm going to love it."

And she said, "Well, I wanted to call you and tell you I was going to bring it but I just happened to be out this way." Imagine happening to be out near me with tuna fish! She said, "Oh, well, now let me get my car keys out," and she pulls open her pocketbook and she dives in this way, you know, and said, "You know, I can never find my car keys." I said, "I know exactly what you mean." So she said, "Oh, this is the funniest *thing* you've ever heard of,"—she pulled out a letter—"Oh, I was going to mail this to you! This is my daughter's engagement. . . ." That's just one of them; there are thousands more.

JACK: When you go by Yolande's desk, there are cakes sitting there, all sorts of things, all because somebody's daughter's getting married.

YOLANDE: Speaking of food, you mind if I tell this one? When I was on the *Constitution*, the food editor quit in a—I don't know what was wrong. You remember when we were in the old building, she got mad with something, so she left. At that time I was working in the society department in the morning and the news job in the afternoon. And I would work from three to seven at night. And so the city editor or somebody said, "Well, Yolande, you just do the food page next week until we can get somebody else." Just as they said that, Ralph McGill walked by. I said, "I don't know anything about doing the food section. All I can cook is chicken and cocoa and things like that, and everybody can read those in a magazine." And Ralph McGill said, "What are you talking about, cooking?" I said, "They want me to do the food page," and he said, "Go on, you can write, can't you? You don't have to cook the food you're writing about."

So my vacation came up a little bit later on, and I went to Washington. I just love Washington. While I was up there, I was invited to a party. The Congressional Club had a party for Mrs. Truman. So I thought, "Well, I'll have to get some sort of a story out of this. Congressional Club parties are routine, you know. I'll just try to wedge my way up to Bess Truman and ask her what her favorite dish is." So I finally got up there, and she couldn't have been nicer. She was so glad I came up from Atlanta to her party, and I said I was delighted to come and all that. And she said, "I'll tell you what, my favorite dish of all is Ozark pudding." And I thought, "Oh, isn't that awful . . . Ozark pudding." And I said, "Oh, that's just marvelous." I came back to Atlanta, and in those days we didn't have the computer. We had the hot type, and so I wrote the food section for the next week and made the lead on Mrs. Truman's Ozark pudding—she gave me the recipe. Well, the paper came out and they dropped one ingredient. It took me six weeks to get that in the paper, because something was dropped every week. I think there was a Republican up there setting the type! I had to go up to north Georgia to some group to make a speech one time, and I was telling them the story and I said, "I never want to hear of Ozark pudding again." So, of course, when they served the dessert, it was Ozark pudding.

JACK: What is Ozark pudding?

YOLANDE: Oh, I don't know—it's terrible.

JACK: We don't want to give away too many trade secrets, Yolande; they might cancel subscriptions for that. I remember the food editor, no matter who she was, was called Sally Savor.

YOLANDE: That's the one that left—well, that was one of the ones.

JACK: Sally Forth in Society and Sally Savor in the Food Section. And Harold Martin was right there on the typewriter.

YOLANDE: That's right, and I sat next to Harold Martin a lot of times, and I was so pleased. I thought, "Isn't this great! I'm sitting next to a great reporter." There he sits, and here Jack sits; I'm right in high cotton right now. Bill Fields is out there somewhere.

JACK: Bill's modest; he's not going to stand up.

YOLANDE: Now tell us some of *your* deals.

JACK: No, I've led a very quiet, anonymous life. All I did was answer the telephone and try to stave off libel suits. Yolande's mothers of the brides would call me up, I do remember that, because the announcement hadn't come out; the lady would call up, and they always wanted it in the Sunday paper. They would say, "Everybody in Thomasville reads the Sunday paper and that's where the groom's family is, so it's got to be in the Sunday paper." And then they'd say—this happened more often than you'd believe—"Let me know what day it's coming out, because we don't take the paper. . . ."

YOLANDE: Do you remember that day we were on Forsyth Street and heard a big excitement in the newsroom, and I went back there and the publicity man was in there with Lassie? Poor Lassie—we didn't have air conditioning then; well, some people did but we didn't—poor Lassie was in the news room, sitting on the floor just panting, and the man was telling everybody about her. I think one of Lassie's films was coming out, so I went back, and I just thought Lassie was so cute. I watched all the episodes on TV about her. So then I went back to my desk, and the hallway was right in front of the door of my department, so when the man left with Lassie they went by and I said, "Goodbye, Lassie," and the man said, "Tell her goodbye," and Lassie barked twice! I was just thrilled to death.

JACK: Were you there the night Larsen Farrar decided to kill Lamar Ball?

YOLANDE: Oh, Lord, yes, tell them about it.

JACK: Larsen had been covering police.

YOLANDE: And stole everybody's story!

JACK: Yes, and Lamar Ball, the city editor, decided he needed a little taking down. So he put him on obit, which suited me fine because it got me off obits; I'd been on them for eighteen months. And Farrar thought about it and thought about it and brooded. That night he came into the city room. The *Constitution's* city desk was a little dais, raised like a little altar, and had a railing like a judge's thing. Old Larsen came up and stood in front of Lamar Ball, as some of you may remember, pulled this pistol out of his pocket, stuck it right at him and said, "I'm going to kill you, you so-and-so," and then fainted dead away.

YOLANDE: And the little cooking editor's assistant, Julia, cute little girl from Tampa—this was during the Depression and jobs were hard to find and people would work for next to nothing—this gal called in sick and didn't show up for two or three days, so someone finally went out to check on her to see how she was. She was quite sick, so they called the doctor, and they found she was suffering from malnutrition. She'd been living off Ozark pudding and stuff like that.

JACK: Yolande, as you have seen, is a great speaker, a charming speaker. I've heard her talk on flags, and she used to have a talk on the language of fans. Do you remember that?

YOLANDE: Oh, yes, I have a little book with all sorts of little, choice bits in it, the language of fans, the language of flowers. I wish I'd thought about bringing one of those flags of mine over here today.

JACK: Tell us about your collection.

YOLANDE: Well, one of the flags I have to keep in a suitcase, it's so big. Dick Russell gave it to me one time, and it had flown over the Senate Building in Washington. It is an American flag with forty-eight stars, which is a rare one now. And it is all tattered and torn. It had been out in the weather, you know, and I just cherish it very much. It's a beautiful thing. And then on the stairway that goes upstairs in my house, I have a satin flag that was on my grandfather's casket when he died, and it has gold fringe on it. It's very pretty, but it's getting so old now that I think I'm going to have to take it down.

I have flags—oh, I can't tell you how many!—I went to Indianapolis one time, to a Beta Sigma Phi convention, and one of the features of the convention was to go to the Indianapolis Speedway. I was talking to this man, who was so glad we all came, you know, and he sat down by me, and I said, "This is exciting, isn't it?" And he said, "It certainly is. Where are you from?" "I'm from Atlanta. Do you know, that hotel where I'm staying doesn't serve Coca-Cola? I think that's terrible. I'm going right back home and tell them about it." He said, "Well, I don't think that's very nice, either. We have it out here. Would you like to have one?" I said, "Yes." He went out and came back with a Coca-Cola. He said, "By the way, you sound like you are a lot of fun. Would you like to have a ride with me around the race track?" I said, "No, thanks!" And do you know who that man was? He was Wilbur Shaw, one of the top racers in the International's history. And he gave me a flag, one of the checkered flags. When we left there that day to go back to the hotel, he looked at me and he said, "Well, you've got your Coke and you've got your flag, but you didn't get to ride, so it's not complete. . . ." I said, "I'll come back. . . ."

JACK: Well, Yola, you were great.

YOLANDE: You were, too, darling.

Index to Names

Index to Places

PHOTO CREDITS

Atlanta Historical Society—88, 104, 133, 138, 147, 155, 161.

Atlanta Journal and Constitution—4, 26, 56, 59, 63, 76, 99, 111, 119, 244.

Benton, Joe—52.

Bond, Warren L.—164.

Courtesy of Alpha Delta Pi Sorority—129.

Courtesy of Mrs. Vann Platter—114.

Downs, Billy—48, 81.

Pugh, Charles—94.

Sutlive, Carey—143.

Swindler, Lanna—22.

Thompson, Ed—68.

Trout, Charles E.—151.

Wilson, Bill—72.

ILLUSTRATIONS

Baldowski, Cliff—209.

Erickson, Lou—170.